# AMERICAN NATURE GUIDES
## INSECTS

# AMERICAN NATURE GUIDES
# INSECTS

GEORGE C. McGAVIN

Illustrated by

RICHARD LEWINGTON

SMITHMARK

This edition first published in 1992 by
SMITHMARK Publishers Inc.,
112 Madison Avenue, New York 10016

Published in England by Dragon's World Ltd,
Limpsfield and London

Editor  Diana Steedman
Designer  James Lawrence
Editorial Director  Pippa Rubinstein
Art Director  Dave Allen

SMITHMARK Books are available for bulk purchase for sales
promotions and premium use.
For details write or telephone the Manager of Special Sales,
SMITHMARK Publishers, Inc.,
112 Madison Avenue
New York, New York 10016. (212) 532-6600

ISBN 0 8317 6951 3

Printed in Singapore

# Contents

# Introduction

Insects are the most successful animals that have ever existed on Earth and have been around for just over 400 million years. Of the nearly one and a half million described species of all animals, just over 930,000 of them are insects. Thousands of new insect species are described every year and recent estimates from work in the world's diminishing rainforests indicate that there are may be several million undescribed species. From the hottest deserts to the polar tundras, from brackish pools to the highest peaks, insects are to be found everywhere. Abundant not only in species, it has been estimated that at any time, on every square mile of land surface, there are thousands of millions of insect individuals.

Why are they so successful? Insects are small and can therefore occupy small ecological niches. A tree may support very few mammal and bird species but can provide a living for hundreds of insect species. Insects reproduce very quickly and can rapidly adjust to environmental changes. It has been calculated that if one pair of pomace flies (Drosophilidae) were to breed free from disease or predation for one year, the resultant progeny, if crammed together 1000 to the cubic inch, would form a ball with a diameter equal to the distance of the Sun from the Earth (93 million miles).

Living organisms can be placed in one of five major groupings or kingdoms. They are the bacteria, the blue-green algae, the fungi, the plants and the animals.

What are the characteristics that distinguish insects from all other animals? Insects have a tough, protective exoskeleton, three pairs of jointed legs, a body divided into three main regions (head, thorax and abdomen), wings (in most) and external mouthparts.

The tough, waterproof exoskeleton of insects has been moulded throughout the course of evolution to provide special mechanisms for running, burrowing, jumping, flying, swimming, prey and food capture, singing and a host of other functions. It may be cryptically or brightly coloured, it may be variously textured and it can be made strong enough to cut through metals and timber or as delicate as gold leaf. The evolution of flight has been a major factor in the success of the insects, allowing them to colonize new habitats and escape from their enemies.

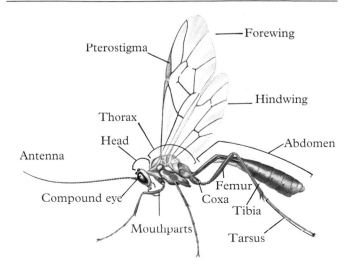

For all their diversity, insects show a remarkable consistency in basic body plan. The first section, the head, is formed from six fused segments and carries the compound eyes, the antennae and the mouthparts. The mouthparts may be modified according to diet, allowing the sucking or lapping of liquids or the chewing and grinding of solid foods. The next section, the thorax, is the powerhouse of the insect and comprises three segments, each bearing a pair of legs. The posterior two thoracic segments usually each bear a pair of wings. The last section or abdomen, usually of 11 segments, contains the digestive and reproductive organs and carries the genitalia. The external genitalia are complex, three-dimensional structures which will only allow mating between the sexes of the same species.

## Why study insects?

Setting aside their supremacy in terms of species diversity and biomass, insects are essential components of every single food chain. Without them, life on this planet, as it exists today, would cease. Insects have an enormous impact on man and every other living organism. As pollinators of plants, scavengers of dead and decaying organic material, recyclers of nutrients and as a source of food to animals (and some plants), insects are of vital importance. Man obtains honey, waxes, silk, dyes, shellac and pharmaceutical products from them and uses them as agents of pest and weed control. Our understanding of genetics, evolution, ecology and many other fields has benefited immeasurably from the study of these creatures. Engineers and architects have much to learn from the world of insects, for in it we find myriad ingenious solutions to life in hostile and changing environments.

Insects eat all manner of organic matter, from nectar to blood, fungi to flesh and plants to petroleum. No plant species is immune from attack. In parts of Africa, nearly 75 per cent of man's crops are lost to the insect multitudes. An average-sized swarm of desert locusts (*Schistocerca gregaria*), containing thousands of millions of individuals and extending over hundreds of square miles, may eat four times as much food in a day as would be consumed by the human population of New York or Greater London. Worldwide, annual crop losses may be 15 per cent or higher. Besides eating our food and that of other animals, our stored products, wooden buildings, fabrics and artefacts, many insects are carriers or vectors of serious plant, animal and human diseases. Among the many hundreds of diseases borne by insects and caused by viruses, bacteria, spirochaetes, rickettsias, protozoans, roundworms and fungi, perhaps the best known is malaria, responsible for around two million human deaths each year.

It is a sobering thought that if just one group of insects, such as the honeybees (Apidae), were removed from the Earth, the destruction of all terrestrial ecosystems would be rapid. Shamefully, through human overpopulation, pollution, forest clearance and wetland drainage, it is virtually certain that the Earth will lose up to half of *all* its animal and plant species well within the next century. If man were removed, the fate of Earth's plants and animals would be decided by a more natural selection.

**The scope of the book**
The world is divided into six major zoogeographical regions: the Ethiopian, Oriental, Australian, Neotropical, Nearctic and Palaearctic. Together, the Nearctic (America north of Mexico) and Palaearctic (Europe and Asia) form a vast area known as the Holarctic region. This area is the northern hemisphere from about 30°N to the North Pole.

The Class Insecta is divided into 28 Orders. Each Order is subdivided into many hundreds of families, each containing anything from one to many thousands of species. The reader is introduced to just some of the more common or more important families occurring across the Holarctic region. To assist in identifying to which Order an insect might belong, use the following diagnoses of the insect Orders.

# The Insect Orders

This section gives the main diagnostic features that will enable the reader to identify most insects encountered to the level of Order. For each Order, the common name, scientific name and numbers recorded from the World, North America (NA) and United Kingdom (UK) are given. For some groups, World numbers are a best estimate and in many groups, the real total will be much higher. Three Orders, Zoraptera, Grylloblattodea and Embioptera are omitted as they are very small groups and rarely encountered.


**CLASS Insecta**
**Subclass I: Apterygota**
Primitively wingless. Do not undergo metamorphosis (ametabolous) and are considered the most primitive of all insects. The young stages resemble the adults in all respects except size and sexual maturity. Moulting may continue after sexual maturity is reached. This Subclass has two Orders.

Bristletails   Archaeognatha (p16)
World–280; NA–25; UK–7
Small; spindle-shaped, almost cylindrical; can jump; body has pigmented scales; eyes large, touching; antennae long, thread-like, multi-segmented; chewing jaws with a single hinge point; thorax 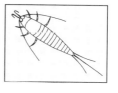 arched; abdomen has 3 terminal filaments of which the middle one is longest and pairs of ventral styles (accessory locomotory organs) on most segments.

Silverfish   Thysanura (p17)
World–330; NA–20; UK–2
Small; elongate, oval and slightly flattened; body with or without scales or pigment-ation; eyes small or absent, not touching; antennae long, multi-segmented; chewing jaws with 2 hinge points; thorax not 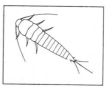 arched; abdomen has 3 terminal filaments of nearly the same length and pairs of walking styles on most segments.

## Subclass II: Pterygota

Winged insects, although secondary loss of wings occurs in some groups.

**Division I: Exopterygota**. In these Orders, the young stages are called nymphs and look very similar to the adults. Their wings develop on the outside of the body (exopterygote) and their metamorphosis is called simple or incomplete (hemimetabolous).

Mayflies   Ephemeroptera (p18–20)
World–2500; NA–611; UK–46
Medium-sized, delicate, elongate, nearly cylindrical body; head with short bristle-like antennae, large eyes; vestigial, chewing mouthparts; 1 pair of triangular front wings and smaller, rounded,

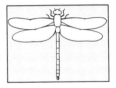

hind wings; wing venation complex; abdomen slender with 2 or 3 long terminal filaments.

Dragonflies & Damselflies
Odonata (p21–24)
World–4900; NA–425; UK–45
Generally large; biting and chewing mouthparts; head, large and mobile; eyes very large; antennae short, bristle-like; 2 pairs of narrow, richly veined, equal or nearly equal-sized wings; legs directed forward; abdomen long, cylindrical.

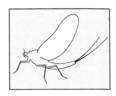

Cockroaches   Blattodea (p25–26)
World–4000; NA–50; UK–8
Medium to large-sized; body flattened, oval; head pointing down, protected by pronotum; eyes large; antennae long, multi-segmented; chewing mouthparts; 2 pairs of wings; front wings hardened and

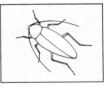

called tegmina; hind wings large, membranous; wing venation mainly longitudinal; legs equal in size, stout, spiny, adapted for running; eggs laid in a tough egg case or ootheca.

Termites   Isoptera (p27)
World–2000; NA–44; UK–0
Polymorphic; mostly small, soft-bodied;
living in social colonies with various castes
(workers, soldiers and reproductives);
head variable according to caste;
mouthparts simple, biting; front part of

head with small pore called the fontanelle; reproductives with
2 pairs of equal-sized wings which are shed; other castes,
wingless; legs, short, equal; abdomen with a pair of short
terminal processes called cerci.

Mantids   Mantodea (p28)
World–1800; NA–20; UK–0
Medium to large-sized; head triangular,
mobile; eyes large; antennae slender,
multi-segmented; biting and chewing
mouthparts; front pair of wings narrow,
thickened; hind wings large,

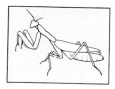

membranous; wing venation complex; front legs large spiny,
raptorial; middle and hind legs normal; eggs laid in an
ootheca.

Angel Insects   Zoraptera
World–24; NA–2; UK–0. Not dealt with in this book.

Rock Crawlers   Grylloblattodea
World–20; NA–10; UK–0. Not dealt with in this book.

Earwigs   Dermaptera (p29–30)
World–1500; NA–20; UK 7
Small to medium-sized; body elongate,
slightly flattened, leathery; eyes medium-
sized or absent; antennae thread-like,
multi-segmented; chewing mouthparts;
front wings tough, short; hind wings very

large, fan-shaped; legs short; abdomen with strong, terminal
forceps which may be very large and curved.

Stoneflies   Plecoptera (p31–33)
World–1600; NA–465; UK–34
Medium-sized; body soft, flattened; eyes
bulging; chewing mouthparts; antennae
thread-like, multi-segmented; 2 pairs of
membranous wings; hind wings broader
than front wings; wing venation complex;

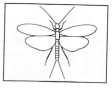

legs strong; abdomen with a pair of terminal cerci.

Grasshoppers & Crickets
Orthoptera (p34–38)
World–19,000; NA–1080; UK–30
Medium to large; body stout or elongate;
eyes medium-sized; antennae multi-
segmented; chewing mouthparts; front
wings, when present, narrow, straight,

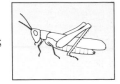

toughened; hind wings, when present, membranous,
fan-shaped; wing venation complex; sound production
common; hind legs often strongly modified for jumping;
abdomen with a pair of short cerci.

Stick Insects   Phasmatodea (p39)
World–2500; NA–29; UK–2
Large; body very elongate and slender,
resembling a twig, or flattened, broad and
leaf-like; chewing mouthparts; antennae
multi-segmented, thread-like or bead-like;
headed domed; front wings tough, small;

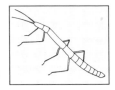

hind wings large, folded fan-like; some species wingless; legs
similar to each other; abdomen with a pair of short cerci.

Web Spinners   Embioptera
World–200; NA–10; UK–0. Not dealt with in this book.

Booklice & Barklice
Psocoptera (p40–41)
World–2600; NA–245; UK–60
Small or minute; body squat, soft; head
mobile, face swollen; eyes large; chewing
and biting mouthparts; antennae long,
thread-like; mostly with 2 pairs of

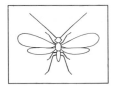

membranous wings; wing venation simple; legs slender,
about equal in size.

Parasitic Lice   Phthiraptera (p42–44)
World–5000; NA–1000; UK–539
Small; ectoparasitic on birds and
mammals; antennae short; eyes small or
absent; mouthparts modified for biting or
sucking; wingless; legs short, stout,
modified for clinging to fur or feathers.

Bugs, Hoppers, Aphids & allies
Hemiptera (p45–74)
World–90,000; NA–9946; UK–1627
Very small to large; body very variable;
mouthparts fused to form a piercing and
sucking tube or rostrum; eyes medium-
sized; antennae variable; usually 2 pairs

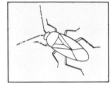

of wings; front wings tougher (sometimes in part) than hind
wings; stink glands and sound-producing organs
sometimes present.

Thrips   Thysanoptera (p75–77)
World–4500; NA–694; UK–159
Small or very small; body elongate,
slender; head elongate; mouthparts
assymetrical, sucking and piercing; eyes
prominent with large facets; wings
narrow, strap-like, hair fringed; wing

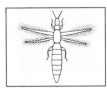

venation reduced; some species wingless; legs short,
of similar size.

**Division II: Endopterygota.** In these Orders, the young
stages are called larvae and look unlike the adults they will
become. Their wings develop internally (endopterygote) and
their metamorphosis is called complete (holometabolous). The
incredible transformation from larval to adult form takes place
within a resting stage or pupa (in butterflies it is known as a
chrysalis). These Orders contain the most advanced insects.

Alderflies & Snakeflies
Megaloptera (p78–79)
World–380; NA–64; UK–6
Medium to large; strong, chewing
mouthparts; eyes large; antennae long,
multi-segmented; thorax sometimes
elongate; 2 pairs of similar-sized wings;

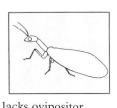

wing venation complex; female sometimes lacks ovipositor.

Lacewings & Antlions
Neuroptera (p80–82)
World–4300; NA–300; UK–54
Small to large; eyes relatively large, often
shining; chewing mouthparts; antennae
long, multi-segmented, thread-like or
clubbed; 2 pairs of similar-sized wings;

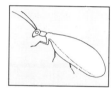

wing venation complex, with veins forked at wing margins.
No abdominal cerci.

Beetles   Coleoptera (p83–108)
World–370,000; NA–24,000; UK–3729
Very small to very large; body variable;
biting and chewing mouthparts, directed
forward; antennae moderately sized,
usually with less than 12 segments;
2 pairs of wings, front pair called wing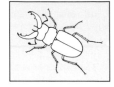
cases or elytra, which are rigid, tough and not used for flying,
hind wings membranous.

Strepsipterans   Strepsiptera (p109)
World–532; NA–109; UK–15
Very small or minute; females, endo-
parasitic on insects, wingless, grub-like;
males with large, transverse head, bulging
eyes, very small non-functional front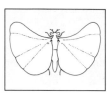
wings, large fan-shaped hind wings with a few radiating veins.

Scorpionflies   Mecoptera (p110–111)
World–500; NA–68; UK–4
Small to medium-sized; body elongate,
slender; head produced downwards;
chewing mouthparts; antennae
thread-like, variable; 2 pairs of
similarly-sized, membranous wings;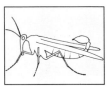
wing venation complex; abdomen of males sometimes with
bulbous, upturned genitalia.

Fleas   Siphonaptera (p112)
World–2000; NA–325; UK–57
Small to minute; wingless; ectoparasitic
on birds and mammals; body tough,
flattened sideways, streamlined; antennae
short, in grooves; mouthparts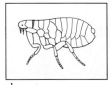
piercing and sucking; eyes small, simple or absent;
legs short, stout; hind legs modifed for leaping.

True Flies or Two-winged Flies
Diptera (p113–146)
World–119,500; NA–16,914; UK–5950
Minute to medium-sized; body variable;
antennae long, multi-segmented, short or
very short, bristle-like, reduced; mouth-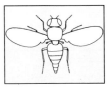
parts for lapping or sucking liquids,
sometimes piercing; 1 pair membranous wings, venation
variable; hind wings greatly modified to form tiny
balancing organs called halteres.

Caddisflies   Trichoptera (p147–149)
World–7000; NA–1261; UK–192
Small to medium-sized; body slender,
moth-like; eyes large; mouthparts reduced
or vestigial; 2 pairs of similarly sized wings;
body and wings covered with hairs and
sometimes scales; legs long, slender.

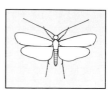

Butterflies & Moths
Lepidoptera (p150–173)
World–165,000; NA–11,286; UK–2495
Very small to very large; body and both
sides of both pairs of wings covered with
minute, overlapped scales; antennae
multi-segmented, variable; eyes large;

mouth-parts usually as sucking proboscis (coiled at rest);
legs well developed, sometimes front pair reduced; hind wings
weakly coupled to front wings in flight.

Sawflies, Wasps, Bees & Ants
Hymenoptera (p174–201)
World–120,000; NA–18,000; UK–6641
Minute to large; body elongate, variable,
usually with constricted waist; eyes large;
chewing mouthparts; 2 pairs of membranous wings, front pair usually larger;

wing venation reduced, simple; hind and front wings strongly
joined, in flight, by tiny hooks on the leading edge of the hind
wing; legs long, variable; some live in social colonies.

The totals for the numbers of insect species are as follows:
World–931,966; NA–87,023; UK–21,709.

# Abbreviations

BL

BL = body length

WS

WS = wingspan

# The Insect Families

The species illustrated, in most cases, occur in North America and the United Kingdom and show the typical appearance of members of their respective families. In a few cases, no single species is truly holarctic in distribution but similar-looking members of the same genus can be found on both sides of the Atlantic. Body lengths and wingspans are given as a guide for northern hemisphere species. World species numbers are best estimates. Worldwide distribution means species belonging to the family are recorded from all zoogeographical regions.

## Jumping Bristletails

**Order** Archaeognatha
**Family** Machilidae
**Body length** up to 12mm (½in)
**Distribution** Worldwide
**Number of species** World–250; NA–14; UK–7

**Identification** Machilids are elongate and usually brownish in colour and their bodies are covered with patterns of scales. They are similar in appearance to the silverfish (Lepismatidae) but are more cylindrical and have a humped thorax. The compound eyes are large and touch each other on top of the head. The end of the abdomen bears three tail-like filaments.
**Habitat** Some species live in grassy or wooded areas, under stones, rock and in leaf litter and detritus, while others are coastal. *Petrobius maritimus* is commonly found running over rocks close to the sea.
**Biology** These insects are quite active and jump when disturbed. They feed mainly on algae but will also eat mosses, lichens and a variety of decaying organic materials. They can be collected most easily at night and move towards light.
**Economic importance** Jumping Bristletails are of no known economic importance.

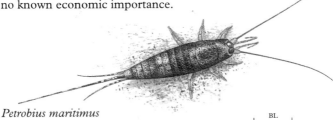

*Petrobius maritimus*

BL

16

# Silverfish and Firebrats

**Order**  Thysanura
**Family**  Lepismatidae
**Body length**  8–20mm (¼–¾in)
**Distribution**  Worldwide
**Number of species**  World–200; NA–13; UK–2

**Identification**  These insects are slender, slightly flattened and elongate. They can be brown or tan in colour and are usually covered in greyish or silvery scales. The compound eyes are small and widely separated. The posterior end of the abdomen bears three tail-like filaments.

**Habitat**  Most species live outdoors, under stones, in caves, among debris and in ant nests. Some species are closely associated with human habitation. Of these species, the Silverfish, *Lepisma saccharina,* prefers cool, damp microhabitats while the Firebrat, *Thermobia domestica,* can be found in bakeries, kitchens and similar places, often near hot pipes and ovens.

**Biology**  Nocturnal and fast-running, silverfish are mostly omnivorous. The domestic species feed on a wide range of starchy materials, such as spilled flour, starched damp textiles, book bindings and wallpaper paste. Spiders are the principal natural enemies of silverfish although they are also attacked by some protozoans and members of the Order Strepsiptera.

**Economic importance**  The presence of silverfish in habitations can indicate poor food-handling practices or damp conditions. Libraries can sometimes suffer serious book or archival damage due to the activities of these small insects. The pest species are cosmopolitan and, in general, the distribution of the family has been greatly extended through the activities of man.

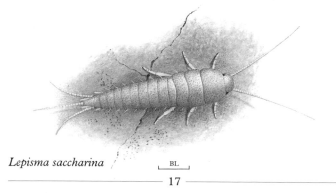

*Lepisma saccharina*                    BL

# Small Mayflies

**Order** Ephemeroptera
**Family** Baetidae
**Body length** 3–12mm (½in), mostly 4–7mm (¼in)
**Distribution** Nearly worldwide
**Number of species** World–800; NA–147; UK–14

**Identification** These mayflies usually have two pairs of wings but in some species the hind wings can be reduced or absent. The front wings are elongate and oval with reduced venation. They may be variously coloured, from light to dark brown or black with light yellowish, grey or white markings. The eyes of males are divided into upper and lower portions. The posterior end of the abdomen carries two very long tails.
**Habitat** Common in a wide range of aquatic habitats. They are rarely found far from streams, rivers, ditches, ponds and lakes. Some species can tolerate polluted water. Of all the mayfly families, these species are found at higher altitudes and latitudes than any others.
**Biology** The aquatic nymphs are herbivorous and can be found among vegetation or under stones and debris. They are active swimmers and climb about on submerged plants but will avoid bright light. Adult females will enter the water, even going through waterfalls to lay their eggs on rocks. *Cloeon dipterum* gives birth to nymphs not eggs. The females will remain hidden in vegetation while their eggs develop inside their bodies. The young nymphs are dropped into the water below.
**Economic importance** These insects are an important food source for freshwater fishes and the adults are modelled by anglers as lures.

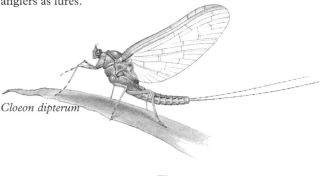

*Cloeon dipterum*

WS

# Stream or Flatheaded Mayflies

**Order** Ephemeroptera
**Family** Heptageniidae
**Body length** 4–15mm (¼–½in), mostly 10mm (⅝in)
**Distribution** Worldwide except Australia
**Number of species** World–550; NA–133; UK–11

**Identification** The adults are mostly dark brown with clear wings. Some species can be yellow or reddish-brown with black, white or yellow markings. The wing venation is distinctive and in many species is dark brown. The eyes of males are not divided into upper and lower portions. The posterior end of the abdomen carries two long tails.

*Rhithrogena semicolorata*

**Habitat** These mayflies are usually associated with fast-flowing water such as mountain streams, although some species can be found around ponds and the margins of lakes.

**Biology** The aquatic nymphs live under stones or logs and sometimes in submerged vegetation or bottom debris. They have flattened heads and bodies and are dark coloured. The nymphs of some species are poor swimmers and cling to the substrate by means of a gill holdfast but many are active. The nymphs of most species feed on algae but some are carnivorous.

**Economic importance**
Important as freshwater fish food and as models for fishing lures.

# Prongill Mayflies

**Order** Ephemeroptera
**Family** Leptophlebiidae
**Body length** 4–14mm (¼–⅝in), mostly 8–10mm (¼–⅜in)
**Distribution** Worldwide
**Number of species** World–600; NA–70; UK–6

**Identification** The colour of the adults is variable from light to dark brown. The wing venation is more or less complete with dark brown longitudinal veins in most species. The eyes of males are strongly divided, the upper area having large facets. The posterior end of the abdomen bears three long tails which may be obviously longer than the whole body.
**Habitat** These insects are found near slow-flowing streams and lake margins.
**Biology** The nymphs of this widely distributed and common group prefer to live in crevices under stones and logs or in debris. They are herbivorous or omnivorous and will avoid light.
**Economic importance** Important as the food of freshwater fishes and as models for fishing lures.

*Leptophlebia marginata*

WS

# Narrow-winged Damselflies

**Order** Odonata
**Family** Coenagrionidae
**Wingspan** Mostly 20–45mm (¾–1¾in)
**Distribution** Worldwide, dominant in temperate areas
**Number of species** World–1000; NA–92; UK–12

**Identification** Many species in this large and successful family are very beautifully coloured in shades of light blue with dark markings. Other species may have blue-green or red-brown coloration with dark markings. The adults are slender or very slender, weak fliers and rest horizontally with their clear wings folded together over the body. In most species there is sexual dimorphism in body colour, the males being more brightly coloured. The small dark mark on the wings, called the pterostigma, is diamond-shaped.

**Habitat** These damselflies occur in a great variety of habitats, mainly along streams but also around ponds and swampy areas. Several species may be found in the same area, flying low over still water.

**Biology** The slender nymphs are of variable colour and can be found climbing about on vegetation in slow or standing water looking for prey. They have three slender gill filaments arising from the end of their abdomens, the middle one being the longest. Two common and cosmopolitan genera are *Ischnura* and *Enallagma*.

**Economic importance** There are no pest species in this family.

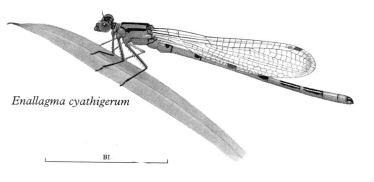

*Enallagma cyathigerum*

BL

# Spread or Stalk-winged Damselflies

**Order** Odonata
**Family** Lestidae
**Wingspan** 32–64mm (1¼–2½in )
**Distribution** Worldwide
**Number of species** World–200; NA–18; UK–2

**Identification** These relatively large damselflies are usually metallic blue, bronze or green in colour. They are quite robust and, when at rest on plant stems, they hold their bodies nearly vertical with their wings slightly apart. The wings are clear with an elongate or rectangular pterostigma and appear to be on stalks.
**Habitat** Adults are mostly found around still water, swamps, boggy places, drainage ditches, acidic pools or lakes.
**Biology** These damselflies can be found sunning themselves on vegetation at the margins of their habitat. The majority of species belong to the cosmopolitan genus *Lestes*. The elongate, slender, predacious nymphs have terminal abdominal gills and elongate mouthparts and are usually found among vegetation in still water.
**Economic importance** Lestids are of no economic significance.

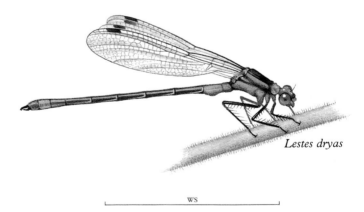

*Lestes dryas*

WS

# Hawkers and Darners

**Order** Odonata
**Family** Aeshnidae
**Wingspan** 55–110mm (2¼–4⅜in), mostly 65–90mm
(2½–3⅝in)
**Distribution** Worldwide
**Number of species** World–500; NA–34; UK–8

**Identification** This family includes some of the largest and
most powerful of the world's dragonflies. They are robust
insects and usually dark coloured with striking blue or green
markings. The eyes are large and touch each other on top of
the head. Some species may be very hairy. The abdomen is
elongate and slender and the thorax is very stout and thick.
The wings have a narrow, elongate pterostigma.
**Habitat** They are mostly found near still waters that have a
large amount of emergent vegetation. Some species may be
found flying far from water along tracks and hedgerows and in
urban areas.
**Biology** Adult aeshnids are fast fliers and some may be very
inquisitive, investigating anything moving in their territory.
The nymphs have large eyes and slender, cylindrical bodies
and can be found living among weed or crawling on the
bottom among debris in search of their prey. Dragonfly
nymphs have internal rectal gills as opposed to the external
abdominal gills of the damselflies. *Aeshna* and *Anax* are two
common cosmopolitan genera, *Brachytron* is typical of the
northern hemisphere.
**Economic importance**
Some species can be
pests around honey bee
hives and can kill large
numbers of workers and
drones.

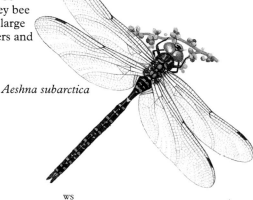

*Aeshna subarctica*

ws

# Common Skimmers and Darters

**Order** Odonata
**Family** Libellulidae
**Wingspan** 20–100mm (¾–4in), mostly 45-75mm (1¾–3in)
**Distribution** Worldwide
**Number of species** World–1250; NA–91; UK–13

**Identification** Members of this large group are the dragonflies commonly seen around ponds and boggy places. Their flight is fast and unpredictable with short periods of hovering. They are colourful but few species have a metallic sheen. Some species show sexual dimorphism in their colour patterns, the bodies of males often having a pale blue, powdery appearance. The wingspan is noticeably longer than the body length. Many species have dark bands or other markings on the wings. The large eyes always touch on top of the head. The bases of the hind wings appear very rounded.
**Habitat** Libellulids are mainly found flying over still water in a variety of habitats, ranging from dense forest to arid areas.
**Biology** This family represents a large proportion of all Odonata. They are variable in many aspects of their biology. Adult males are very territorial and will command their patch from a perch on an exposed plant stem or twig. The predacious, aquatic nymphs are short, stocky, flattened and hunt for their food in the bottom mud or detritus. The genera *Libellula* and *Sympetrum* are holarctic, *Orthetrum* is cosmopolitan.
**Economic importance** There are no serious pest species, but there have been reports of these dragonflies catching and eating honey bees.

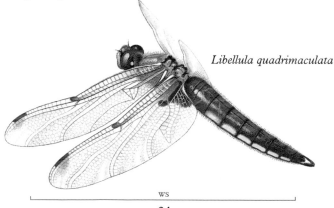

*Libellula quadrimaculata*

WS

# American Cockroaches

**Order** Blattodea
**Family** Blattidae
**Body length** 25–45mm (1–1¾in)
**Distribution** Worldwide
**Number of species** World–600; NA–6; UK–3

**Identification** The members of this family are oval in shape with flattened bodies. The head is not visible from above as it is concealed by the pronotum. In general they are brown, reddish-brown or blackish-brown with darker or paler markings. Many species have a glossy or shiny appearance. The antennae are long and slender. The underside of the middle and hind legs are spiny.

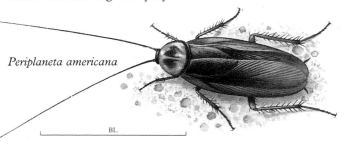

*Periplaneta americana*

BL

**Habitat** These cockroaches can be found in the wild and in habitations. Many species prefer warm humid conditions in houses, restaurants, bakeries, warehouses, sewers and rubbish dumps. Some species are common around ports and on ships.
**Biology** Blattids mainly feed at night and are attracted to a wide variety of foodstuffs. During the day they hide in cracks and crevices, under floors, behind skirting boards and similar places. They are very active, fast-running and will only fly in very warm environments. Some species emit a foul-smelling liquid. The female American Cockroach (*Periplaneta americana*) can produce up to about 50 egg cases, each containing 12–14 eggs, glued to objects in concealed places.
**Economic importance** Several domestic pests occur in this family. *Periplaneta americana* and *Blatta orientalis* (the Oriental Cockroach) are common cosmopolitan species, particularly in urban slum areas and indicate poor hygiene and food-handling practices, although in warmer parts of the world they are ubiquitous and impossible to eliminate. *Periplaneta americana* has been used extensively for research and teaching purposes.

# German Cockroaches

**Order** Blattodea
**Family** Blattellidae
**Body length** 8–25mm (¼–1in), mostly 15mm (⅜in)
**Distribution** Worldwide
**Number of species** World–1750 ; NA–24; UK–4

**Identification** Most members of this large family of cockroaches are brown to light brown in colour but a few species are olive green. They look shiny and have variable markings of a darker brown on the pronotum and wings. They are similar in general appearance to the Blattidae. The legs are slender and the antennae long. One of the best-known species is the German Cockroach, *Blattella germanica*, which is light brown with two longitudinal, dark brown stripes on the pronotum. Some tropical species may be 100mm(4in) long.

**Habitat** Found outdoors among woodland litter and debris, as well as in houses.

**Biology** These omnivorous insects are very similar in general biology to the Blattidae. Females of *B. germanica* produce an average of five egg cases containing about 40 eggs each. Rather than sticking the egg cases to objects, the female carries the case around, protruding from her body, until just before the eggs are due to hatch. Both sexes of most species are fully-winged but do not readily fly.

**Economic importance** *Blattella germanica* is a major household pest in many areas. Like many cockroaches it was introduced to temperate parts of the world from hotter areas like North Africa. The presence of this species is marked by a characteristic odour which it leaves behind everywhere it goes. In the summer months it can be found outdoors on refuse dumps and similar places where there is a good supply of food.

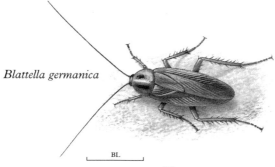

*Blattella germanica*

BL

# Subterranean Termites

**Order** Isoptera
**Family** Rhinotermitidae
**Body length** 6–8mm (¼–⅜in)
**Distribution** Worldwide in warmer regions
**Number of species** World–200; NA–9; UK–0

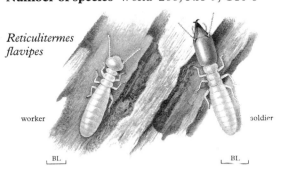

*Reticulitermes flavipes*

worker

soldier

**Identification** The head of these soft-bodied social insects is usually longer than it is broad. The pronotum of all castes (soldiers, workers and reproductives) is rounded at the back and may, in some species, appear almost heart-shaped. Wingless forms are pale in colour. Soldiers have a pale brown head and their mandibles do not have teeth. The winged reproductive forms are black.

**Habitat** The nests are always found in damp soil or in damp timbers in close ground contact. In North America, most species are restricted to warmer southern areas. There are only two species of termite in Europe, *Reticulitermes lucifugus* (this family) and *Kalotermes flavicollis* (Kalotermitidae).

**Biology** Species in this family are social, occurring in colonies of thousands of individuals with distinct castes having separate functions. They feed on wood and use intestinal protozoans to digest the chewed fibres. They always maintain a close contact with the soil and will burrow into tree stumps, roots or timbers in or beneath the surface. They can reach wood not in ground contact by building earth tunnels. Swarms of reproductive individuals appear at intervals. After a short mating flight their wings are shed and some become the kings and queens of new colonies.

**Economic importance** Several species in this group are significant pests, damaging structural and non-structural timbers. In North America, *R. flavipes* is widespread and the most destructive of all termite species.

# Praying Mantids

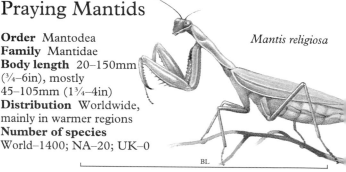

**Order** Mantodea
**Family** Mantidae
**Body length** 20–150mm
(¾–6in), mostly
45–105mm (1¾–4in)
**Distribution** Worldwide,
mainly in warmer regions
**Number of species**
World–1400; NA–20; UK–0

*Mantis religiosa*

BL

**Identification** Members of this, the largest of all the mantid families, are green or brownish-grey in colour. They are easily recognized by the way they sit motionless on vegetation waiting for their next meal. The large front legs are highly modified, mobile and armed with rows of sharp spines for impaling their victims. The common name for these insects comes from the upright position they adopt, with their front legs raised together in an attitude of prayer. The head is triangular, very manoeuvrable and attached to an elongate thorax. It is often said that they are the only insects that can look over their shoulders. The eyes are large and have zones of high acuity.

**Habitat** They occur anywhere on vegetation where there is a good supply of suitable insects.

**Biology** These solitary, highly predacious insects usually have one generation per year. The female, after mating (which the males may or may not survive), lays a couple of hundred eggs surrounded by an egg case or ootheca which has a papery texture. The ootheca is attached to vegetation where the eggs may spend the winter. The European Mantid, *Mantis religiosa*, was introduced to the USA at the turn of this century and is now common in many parts of the country.

**Economic importance** These insects have been sold in garden shops as a good way of keeping down garden pests. The trouble is that they do not distinguish between pest and beneficial species and sometimes can be a pest themselves by eating large numbers of honey bees. They are, however, fascinating and instructive to keep at home, and in a suitably baited trap, will dispose of all household flies. They will try to bite if handled roughly but are not in the least dangerous.

# Striped Earwigs

**Order** Dermaptera
**Family** Labiduridae
**Body length** Up to 35mm (1⅜in)
**Distribution** Worldwide, mainly in warmer areas.
**Number of species** World–75; NA–1; UK–1

**Identification** These rather primitive earwigs are fairly robust, reddish-brown in colour and sometimes fully-winged. The largest European species and the only one in this family to occur in the USA is *Labidura riparia*. It is easily recognized by its large size and the longitudinal dark brown stripes on the pronotum and wing cases. The pincers are large and not as curved as in the Forficulidae (p.30).
**Habitat** Striped earwigs can be found hiding under debris during the day and are common on seashores, the banks of rivers and in refuse dumps.
**Biology** *Labidura riparia* is typical of the group. It is partly or wholly predacious, nocturnal and prefers sandy areas where it may dig tunnels and burrow to lay eggs. These earwigs can protect themselves by discharging a foul-smelling fluid from abdominal glands. Some species can project a quantity of the liquid over a short distance.
**Economic importance** Labidurids are of little or no importance, but males can give a pinch with their powerful terminal forceps.

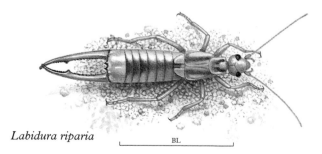

*Labidura riparia*                    BL

# Common Earwigs

**Order** Dermaptera
**Family** Forficulidae
**Body length** 12–25mm (½–1in)
**Distribution** Worldwide
**Number of species** World–465; NA–4; UK–3

**Identification** Forficulids are dark brown or blackish-brown earwigs with pale legs and thread-like antennae. The hardened wing cases are small, pale brown and, as in all winged earwigs, cover the delicate and intricately folded, fan-shaped hind wings. The body is flattened and the abdomen bears a pair of terminal forceps. The forceps of males are very curved while those of the females are much straighter. The commonest species is the cosmopolitan earwig *Forficula auricularia*.
**Habitat** These earwigs are free-living in ground litter, in soil, under bark or in rocky crevices.
**Biology** Forficulids are usually nocturnal and omnivorous although some prefer plant material. Common earwigs rarely fly, perhaps due to the difficulty of folding their hind wings but more probably because, like other earwigs, they have a lifestyle that does not demand flight very often. As with all earwigs, the forceps are used for courtship and defence. Some species show primitive maternal care, females standing guard over their egg batches to ward off predators.
**Economic importance** Species in this family can be garden and crop pests. Since its introduction to the USA from Europe in the early 1900s, *F. auricularia* has spread widely and, when present in large numbers, has caused occasional, but substantial, damage to a variety of vegetable, cereal and fruit crops. More usually, these insects are garden pests, destroying ornamental blooms by chewing through the bases of petals.

*Forficula auricularia*

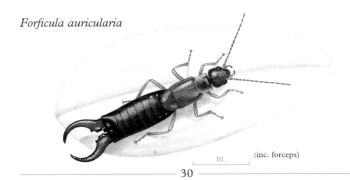

BL

(inc. forceps)

# Spring Stoneflies

**Order** Plecoptera
**Family** Nemouridae
**Body length** 6–15mm (¼–⅝in), mostly under 10mm (⅜in)
**Distribution** Northern hemisphere
**Number of species** World–400; NA–58; UK–11

**Identification** Black or brown in general body colour, these stout-bodied stoneflies have a generalized and uniform wing venation. The abdomen carries a pair of very short, terminal tails or cerci.

**Habitat** Spring stoneflies can be found around the fast-flowing rocky streams where their nymphs live.

**Biology** The aquatic, immature stages are darkish-brown, dull and are covered with many spines and hairs. They are herbivorous and prefer small streams with sandy bottoms where they feed on leaves, algae, diatoms or detritus. The vast majority of the American species belong to the genus *Nemoura*. This genus and the genus *Amphineura* are common across the northern hemisphere.

**Economic importance** There are no pest species in this family but many species are important as freshwater fish food and are used by fishermen as bait.

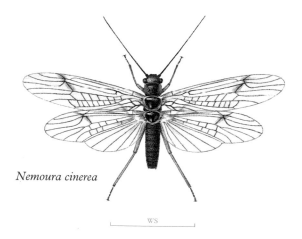

*Nemoura cinerea*

WS

# Small Winter Stoneflies

**Order** Plecoptera
**Family** Capniidae
**Body length** 5–25mm (¼–1in), mostly under 12mm (½in)
**Distribution** Northern hemisphere
**Number of species** World–250; NA–129; UK–3

**Identification** Most species in this family are blackish in colour. The wings, which have have few cross veins, may be very short in some species. The terminal abdominal tails may be as long as the body.
**Habitat** Adults can be found around small streams or on buildings, tree trunks or stones near the shores of lakes. Capniids are common in colder, more northerly areas.
**Biology** As the common name implies, these stoneflies usually emerge from their watery, nymphal habitats during winter months. Despite prolonged sub-zero temperatures, they can still crawl around, mate and lay eggs. The adults feed on blue-green algae while the nymphs are plant-feeders. The terminal appendages of the nymphs are long. The genus *Capnia* is the largest in the family and common throughout the northern hemisphere.
**Economic importance** There are no pest species, but like other stoneflies they are essential in freshwater ecosystems as fish food.

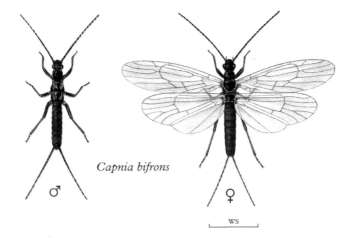

*Capnia bifrons*

♂

♀

ws

# Predatory Stoneflies

**Order** Plecoptera
**Family** Perlodidae
**Body length** 6–25mm (¼–1in)
**Distribution** Northern hemisphere
**Number of species** World–250; NA–98; UK–5

**Identification** The commonest species in this family have yellowish-green bodies and green wings, while other species may be blackish-brown. The pronotum is rectangular in shape and the terminal abdominal tails are long. The males of some species have short wings. Adults stages of many species have non-functional mouthparts and die shortly after emergence and mating.

**Habitat** Commonly found around stony and gravel-bottomed streams. Some species are common in water that is rich in dissolved limestone.

**Biology** The adults are day-flying and some may feed on pollen while their aquatic nymphs may be carnivorous or omnivorous. The nymphs appear waxy-textured and do not have gills. They mainly prefer quieter waters, although some species can be found in faster-flowing streams. Adults usually emerge around late spring or early summer. *Isoperla* is the largest genus in North America.

**Economic importance** These are not pest species.

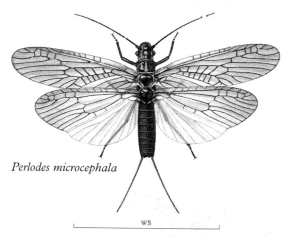

*Perlodes microcephala*

ws

# Long-horned Grasshoppers, Bush Crickets & Katydids

**Order** Orthoptera
**Family** Tettigoniidae
**Body length** 15-75mm (⅝–3in), mostly 35–50mm (1⅜–2in)
**Distribution** Worldwide, mainly tropical
**Number of species** World–5000; NA–243; UK–6

**Identification** Tettigoniids are generally large brownish or greenish insects, although some species may be black, grey or pinkish. Wings, when present, slope down over the sides of the body. The thread-like antennae are usually much longer than the body. The females have distinctive, laterally flattened ovipositors which may be short and curved like a sickle or long like a sabre. In some species the ovipositor can be longer than the body. The hind legs are modified for jumping and are usually very long indeed. Each species has a characteristic song produced by a file and scraper on the front wings rubbing together. The hearing organs are located on the front tibiae.
**Habitat** These insects can be found from ground level to the tree tops in a wide variety of habitats.
**Biology** Most species are plant-feeders, but some are predacious on other insects. Tettigoniids are active from dusk till dawn. It is normally only the males who 'sing' or stridulate but in some species, females occasionally sing as well. Eggs are laid in longitudinal rows inside plant tissues or sometimes in the soil, where they may overwinter. There may be five or six nymphal stages before adulthood is reached. Mimicry of dead or living leaves occurs in some species or they may be cryptically coloured to resemble lichen or other substrates. The family is divided into numerous subfamilies, some of which are given family rank by several authors.
**Economic importance** Many species have pest status and may be very destructive to shrubs, trees and crop plants.

*Metrioptera roeselli*

BL

34

# True Crickets

**Order** Orthoptera
**Family** Gryllidae
**Body length** 4–45mm (¼–1¾in)
**Distribution** Worldwide
**Number of species** World–1800; NA–96; UK–3

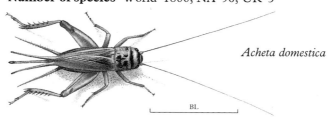

*Acheta domestica*

BL

**Identification** Crickets are rather drably coloured black or shades of brown or green. They resemble tettigoniids in that they have long, thin antennae, stridulatory organs on the front wings and hearing organs on the front legs but differ in that they are somewhat flattened in general shape and the end of the abdomen bears a pair of noticeable, unsegmented cerci. In most gryllids the ovipositor is not flattened from side to side as in the tettigoniids but rather cylindrical or needle-like. The head is rounded and the front wings, when present, sit flat over the back. The hind wings may appear to be rolled up and in many species extend beyond the end of the abdomen. Many species are well known for their songs.

**Habitat** Gryllids can be found in woodlands, meadows, scrub and grasslands. Most species live on the ground and hide under stones, logs or litter while others may be tree-dwelling.

**Biology** The family is divided into several subfamilies, tree crickets, ground crickets, house and field crickets being common groups. In general, eggs are laid singly in the soil or in rows inside plant tissue. Burrowing gryllids may lay masses of eggs underground. Some crickets are active day and night while others are nocturnal. The majority of species are omnivorous or herbivorous but some are particularly fond of aphids and other soft-bodied prey. Peculiar ant-nest-inhabiting species are small, wingless and oval with relatively short, squat hind legs. They feed partly on secretions from their hosts. There may be up to ten nymphal stages.

**Economic importance** There are some pest species of pastures and crops. *Acheta domesticus*, the European House Cricket, has been introduced to the USA and is widespread in houses and bakeries, where it prefers warm locations.

# Mole Crickets

**Order** Orthoptera
**Family** Gryllotalpidae
**Body length** 20–50mm (¾–2in)
**Distribution** Nearly worldwide
**Number of species** World–60; NA–7; UK–1

**Identification** Mole crickets, as the name implies, show superb adaptations to life underground. The body is very robust, cylindrical and covered with very short, velvety hairs. The legs are short and strong. The front legs are particularly modified for digging, being broad and armed with stout teeth. The antennae are short and the wings are short and leathery, covering only about half of the abdomen. The eyes are small and the ovipositor is very short or vestigial. These insects are generally reddish-brown with dark brown or pinkish-brown markings. When viewed from the front, they look remarkably like tiny moles.

**Habitat** Mole crickets burrow in sand or soil near streams, ponds or lakes. The burrows can be up to 200mm(8in) below ground.

**Biology** These fascinating creatures are omnivorous, eating worms and the grubs of other insects as well as gnawing at plant roots. Eggs are laid in an underground chamber and full development through the ten or so nymphal stages may take up to two years. Mole crickets cannot jump but fully-winged species may fly at night and can be attracted to bright lights. The most interesting aspect of their biology is that they construct elaborate, amplifying burrows for singing. The burrows may have twin, exponentially flared horns leading to the surface from a resonant chamber. On a still night, their songs can be heard up to 1km (½ mile) away. The European Mole Cricket *Gryllotalpa gryllotalpa* has been introduced to the USA.

**Economic importance** Mole crickets can damage crops and garden vegetables by chewing roots. In North America, tobacco, peanut and strawberry crops can be affected.

*Gryllotalpa grylloptalpa*

BL

# Short-horned Grasshoppers & Locusts

*Chorthippus brunneus*

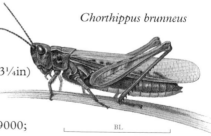

**Order** Orthoptera
**Family** Acrididae
**Body length** 10–80mm (³/₈–3¹/₄in)
Mostly 15–30mm
(⁵/₈–1¹/₄in)
**Distribution** Worldwide
**Number of species** World–9000;
NA–550; UK–11

BL

**Identification** It is hard to generalize about this very large family but most are brown, green or blackish with markings of all colours. Some species are cryptically patterned while others may be very brightly coloured. The antennae are short, and the hind legs are greatly enlarged for jumping and kicking. The females, which are nearly always larger or much larger than the males, have a short ovipositor. Unlike the Gryllidae and the Tettigoniidae, the hearing organs are located at the base of the abdomen. At rest, the large hind wings are folded beneath the narrower and tougher front wings. When disturbed, many species will snap open their wings, displaying vivid colours on the hind wings to frighten their enemies.

**Habitat** Found on the ground and on vegetation, the majority of grasshoppers seen in meadows, hedgerows and other habitats during the summer are acridids.

**Biology** All acridids are foliage-feeders, eating a wide range of plants. They are active during the day and prefer warm or hot conditions. Males sing by rubbing a row of small pegs on the inside face of their hind femora against the hardened edge of the front wings. These grasshoppers can increase to large population densities and many will migrate over long distances. Females lay their eggs in the ground and surround them with a sticky secretion which hardens to form a protective egg pod. There are many important subfamilies which include the spur-throated, slant-faced and band-winged grasshoppers. In North America the spur-throated grasshopper, genus *Melanoplus*, contributes some 300 species to the total fauna.

**Economic importance** Many species are very serious pests, capable of causing enormous crop losses. The Desert Locust of Africa, *Schistocerca gregaria*, probably one of the most damaging insects in the world, belongs to this family.

# Groundhoppers, Grouse Locusts or Pygmy Locusts

**Order** Orthoptera
**Family** Tetrigidae
**Body length** 6–18mm (¼–¾in), mostly around 15mm (⅝in)
**Distribution** Worldwide, mainly warmer regions.
**Number of species** World–1000; NA–29; UK–3

**Identification** These small orthopterans are easily recognized by the peculiar shape of the pronotum. It is extended backwards over the whole of the abdomen and tapers to a point. In many species, the pronotum is strangely contorted to resemble leaves, stones or twigs. The front wings are reduced to small scale-like structures but the hind wings, when present, are usually of normal size and are tucked under the pronotal extension. The legs are short and the femora of the hind legs are stout. In general, the females are slightly larger and more robust than the males. Many species are drab or cryptically coloured to match the mossy or stony substrate.
**Habitat** Groundhoppers are confined to moist woodlands and the margins of bogs and lakes.
**Biology** The biology of these insects is not very well known. Females lay their eggs in loose aggregations in wet soil. Tetrigids feed on algae, mosses, small plants and the organic components of mud. Many are good swimmers while others have semi-aquatic habits. They are active all year round and prefer sunny situations on bare or sparsely covered ground. In temperate regions many species overwinter as nymphs or adults. *Tetrix subulata* is called the Granulated Grouse Locust in North America but is known as the Slender Groundhopper in Europe. It is found in low-lying wet woods and bog margins throughout the year and is pale brownish to blackish in colour.
**Economic importance** Although reasonably common in some areas, very few species are of economic importance.

*Tetrix subulata*    └─ BL ─┘

# Winged Walkingsticks or Stick Insects

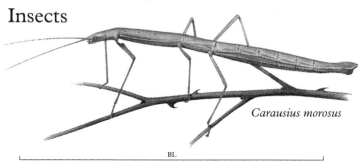

*Carausius morosus*

BL

**Order** Phasmatodea
**Family** Phasmatidae
**Body length** 25–130mm (1–5¼in)
**Distribution** Mainly tropical and oriental
**Number of species** World–600; NA–1; UK–0

**Identification** The body and legs are very long, slender and cylindrical, making these creatures resemble twigs and sticks. Stick insects are generally brown or green but may be blackish or, rarely, metallic blue or green. The head may have two stout spines and the thorax and legs may be spiny or have small warts. The antennae are simple and of variable length. The legs are generally equal in size and are not used for jumping. Stick insects will sway in the breeze to imitate the vegetation or, if disturbed, fall to the ground and remain motionless.
**Habitat** Found generally among grassy vegetation or on the foliage of shrubs and trees.
**Biology** Stick insects are very slow-moving plant-feeders. The nymphs look like the adults but are smaller. They feed mostly at night and camouflage themselves from predators among foliage during the day. Some species have brightly coloured hind wings which may be flashed as a warning, while others may produce repugnant odours. The Phasmatidae is represented in North America by *Aplopus mayeri*, which is common in the south. There are another 31 species in three other families, which are also more common in the warmer southern States. In the UK there are only two species in the Order, belonging to the family Lonchodidae. The Laboratory Stick Insect, *Carausius morosus*, is up to 80mm (3¼in) long.
**Economic importance** Some species in closely related families can defoliate forest trees, some are used as research animals and many exotic species are sold as pets.

# Ectopsocids

**Order** Psocoptera
**Family** Ectopsocidae
**Body length** 1.5–3.5mm (less than ¼in)
**Distribution** Worldwide
**Number of species** World–120; NA–9; UK–1

**Identification** Ectopsocids are very similar in general appearance to narrow booklice. The head is very hairy and the eyes are small. The head and thorax are usually light brown and the abdomen may have dark brown rings. The wings are clear or have a smoky tinge and the venation is generally brown. The antennae are as long as the front wings in males or shorter in females.
**Habitat** These insects may be found in greenhouses all year round, or outside in colonies under dry leaves of various deciduous tree species, or in leaf litter.
**Biology** Ectopsocids eat fungal threads, algae, pollen and other organic matter. They prefer dying leaves where fungal infections are present. Eggs are laid in small groups, covered with silk, on the veins of withering leaves. A single female can lay up to 200 eggs which she covers with silk and detritus. *Ectopsocus briggsi* is typical and nearly cosmopolitan in distribution.
**Economic distribution** Some species are occasionally found in warehouses where foodstuffs are stored but, in general, they are of no importance.

*Ectopsocus briggsi*

WS

# Common Barklice

**Order**  Psocoptera
**Family**  Psocidae
**Body length**  1–6mm (less than ¼in)
**Distribution**  Worldwide
**Number of species**  World–500; NA–62; UK–12

**Identification**  Most common barklice are of drab appearance, being dull brown with or without paler markings. The wings may be tinged with brown or have rows of spots or patches. The antennae are brown in most genera. Most of the barklice encountered in general habitats will be members of this family.

**Habitat**  Common barklice are commonly found on the bark, twigs and branches of various trees, on the foliage of coniferous species and on rocks.

**Biology**  Although the majority of species eat pollen, algae, fungi, lichen and plant material, some may be scavengers. Often, herds of many hundreds of these insects can be found on tree bark. Their eggs are glued inside crevices and cracks in bark and the life-cycle may take eight to ten weeks in temperate regions. *Psocus, Trichadenotectnum* and *Psococerastis* are among some of the genera occurring in the northern hemisphere.

**Economic importance**  There are no pest species in this family.

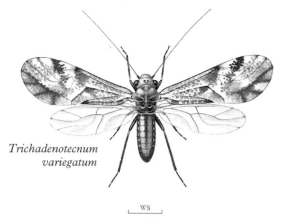

*Trichadenotecnum
variegatum*

WS

# Bird Lice

**Order** Phthiraptera
**Family** Menoponidae
**Body length** 1–6mm (less than ¼in)
**Distribution** Worldwide
**Number of species** World–650; NA–260; UK–146

**Identification** These small, flattened ectoparasites are very pale brown in colour, sometimes with darker markings. The head is large, broadly triangular and expanded behind the eyes. The short antennae are slightly clubbed and can be concealed in grooves on the underside of the head. The abdomen is broadly oval. The legs are short and stout, each with two specially adapted claws for holding on to their host's feathers. The mandibles, or jaws, bite horizontally. Like all parasitic lice, they have no wings.
**Habitat** All are found attached to or inside the feathers of their avian hosts. Some unusual species live inside the mouth pouches of pelicans and cormorants.
**Biology** All the species in this very large family of parasitic lice feed on fragments of skin and feathers which they scrape off with their mandibles. Their diet is augmented by skin secretions and blood. The eggs are glued singly to feathers with a water-insoluble substance. Most species are host-specific, although some attack closely related species. Nymphs are very similar to the adults. In North America some species in the family are called poultry lice.
**Economic importance** Some species are quite serious pests of poultry. The Large Hen or Chicken Body Louse, *Menacanthus stramineus,* and the Shaft Louse, *Menopon gallinae,* are two well-known pest species. Infestations of these species lead to feather loss and reduced host health.

*Menopon gallinae*

# Mammal-chewing Lice

**Order**  Phthiraptera
**Family**  Trichodectidae
**Body length**  1–3mm (less than ⅛in)
**Distribution**  Worldwide
**Number of species**  World–350; NA–137; UK–21

**Identification**  Both sexes are oval in shape and pale brown to dark brown in colour. The abdomen is usually paler with brown markings. The legs are short and stout and each bears a single tarsal claw. The tibiae are broadened towards their ends. The head is not triangular but rather squarish in appearance. The antennae are prominent and have three segments. The mandibles bite vertically.
**Habitat**  These parasitic lice are found on the bodies of their mammalian hosts.
**Biology**  Trichodectids are parasitic on Carnivora and some species specialize on rodents, hyraxes, lorises and cebid monkeys. The biology is very similar to that of other parasitic lice familes. They live in the fur of their hosts and feed on skin fragments, hair, secretions and blood.
**Economic importance**  Some species in this family are pests of domesticated animals. The cattle-biting louse, *Bovicola bovis*, the horse-biting louse, *B. equi*, and the Dog Louse, *Trichodectes canis,* are typical examples. These species can cause severe irritation to their hosts and loss of hair due to scratching. The Dog Louse is known to transmit tapeworms from dog to dog, but no other species is a known disease vector.

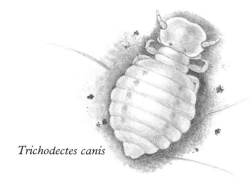

*Trichodectes canis*

⌐⌐ BL

# Body Lice

**Order** Phthiraptera
**Family** Pediculidae
**Body length** 1.5–3.5mm (less than 1/8in)
**Distribution** Worldwide
**Number of species** World–2; NA–1; UK–1

**Identification** These lice have
narrow heads and pear-shaped,
flattened bodies. They are
reddish-brown or pale brown
in colour and differ from the
previous two families in that
the mouthparts are modified
for piercing and sucking, not
chewing. Like all parasitic lice,
they are well adapted to their

*Pediculus humanis*

hosts and have short, strong, inwardly curved legs each armed
with a large claw for grasping.

**Habitat** These lice rarely leave the bodies of their hosts.

**Biology** The family contains one genus, *Pediculus*, with two
species. *Pediculus humanus* has two subspecies on man, (*P.
humanus humanus*, Body Louse, and *P. humanus capitis*, Head
Louse), and also occurs on New World monkeys. The other
species, *P. schaeffi*, is found on gibbons and apes. Human head
and body lice do not appear to differ from each other in any
morphological features but do differ in the area of the body
they use. The Body Louse attaches its eggs to clothing'
especially the seams, and lives in the fibres of the clothing,
leaving to feed on blood and then returning to its hiding place.
Each meal takes a few minutes and they feed at frequent
intervals. The whole life-cycle may take up to five weeks. The
Head Louse lives entirely in hair and attaches its eggs (nits) to
hair shafts with a strong glue. The Head Louse is transmitted
by exchange of head-wear, combs, direct contact and fallen
hair carrying eggs. The Body Louse is transmitted by sharing
infested clothes or bedding. Some authors include the Pubic
Louse, *Pthirus pubis*, in this family but it is correctly placed
with one other species, *P. gorillae*, in the family Pthiridae.

**Economic importance** The Body Louse is a vector of
serious diseases such as typhus, relapsing fever and trench
fever. Infestations occur in crowded and insanitary conditions
and many millions of deaths have been caused by them.
During the Russian Revolution, three million people are
believed to have died from louse-borne typhus.

# Delphacid Planthoppers

**Order** Hemiptera
**Family** Delphacidae
**Body length** 2–9mm (³⁄₈in), mostly around 5mm (¹⁄₄in)
**Distribution** Worldwide
**Number of species** World–1800; NA–145; UK–70

**Identification** These planthoppers are mostly brown or greenish and have an elongate body which is nearly parallel-sided. The head is usually short but may be as long as the body in some species. The antennae are short and simple. Most species have short-winged and fully-winged forms. The females have a relatively large, curved ovipositor. Males and females of some species may look very different. The most distinctive feature of these insects is the presence of a large, flat, articulated spur at the end of the tibiae of the hind legs.
**Habitat** Delphacids are common everywhere in grassy areas, meadows, pastures and woodland margins.
**Biology** All species are plant-feeders, nymphs and adults using their sucking mouthparts to ingest plant fluids. Grasses and sedges are the main host plants but other types of vegetation can be attacked by some species. Eggs are laid inside plant tissues.
**Economic importance** Some species can be serious pests of crop plants, especially in tropical and subtropical regions. Many are vectors of viral plant diseases. *Peregrinus maidis*, the Corn Hopper, is a vector of maize stripe virus and destructive throughout North America and other parts of the world. The Sugarcane Leafhopper, *Perkinsiella saccharicida*, was introduced by accident from northern Queensland to Hawaii, where it caused great damage. It was controlled by the use of another insect, a small bug that preyed on the eggs of the leafhopper. The well-known Asian Rice Brown Planthopper, *Nilaparvata lugens*, is a member of this family.

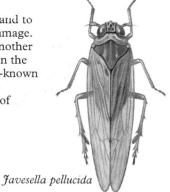

*Javesella pellucida*

BL

# Froghoppers

**Order** Hemiptera
**Family** Cercopidae
**Body length** 5–20mm (¼–¾in), mostly under 14mm (⅝in)
**Distribution** Worldwide, mainly tropical
**Number of species** World–1400; NA–33; UK–1

**Identification** Froghoppers are active jumpers and are very similar in appearance to the spittle bugs. The head is narrower than the pronotum which can look vaguely hexagonal in shape with the front edge nearly straight. They are usually brown or grey but some species can be black with vivid red or orange markings.
**Habitat** Cercopids can be found on a variety of plants in well-vegetated areas, meadows, scrub and woods.
**Biology** Like the spittle bugs, the nymphs produce a frothy substance from their hind ends which serves to reduce evaporation and protect them from some predators. All species are plant-feeders, sucking juices from phloem vessels in leaves and stems. Many species have subterranean nymphs which suck juices from roots. *Cercopis vulnerata* is a typical species. Many authorities consider the spittle bugs (Aphrophoridae) to be a subfamily of this family.
**Economic importance** Several species are pests, damaging plants by their feeding activities. Brown lesions on leaves are produced by their toxic saliva (froghopper blight).

*Cercopis vulnerata*

└─ BL ─┘

# Spittle Bugs

**Order** Hemiptera
**Family** Aphrophoridae
**Body length** 6–12mm (¼–½in)
**Distribution** Worldwide
**Number of species** World–850; NA–23; UK–9

## Identification

*Philaenus spumarius*

Members of this family are very similar to froghoppers but the front edge of the pronotum is arched or curved forwards. The eyes are wider than they are long (in froghoppers they are as wide as long). The hind tibiae have one or two strong spines and a circle of smaller spines at their ends. They are active jumpers. Members of this family are very variable in colour, pale to dark brown with mottled lighter shades and bands. Some species have many colour forms.

**Habitat** Spittle bugs are common everywhere on a wide range of woody and herbaceous plants.

**Biology** The nymphs of some species live underground but most are to be found feeding on leaves, shoots and stems. The pale green or brown nymphs are easily recognized by the frothy covering which is produced by the nymphs blowing their watery waste through a modified anus. Air is introduced through a special valve and a glandular secretion makes the resultant foam long lasting. The nymphs are very soft and cannot jump. Some birds have learned to pull these tiny insects from their protective froth and some parasitic wasps are able to locate and parasitize them.

**Economic importance** Some species have minor pest status. In North America two species attack pines. The Meadow Spittle Bug, *Philaenus spumarius*, is common to the northern hemisphere and feeds on a wide range of wild and cultivated plants. It has many colour varieties and can cause considerable damage to clovers.

# Cicadas

**Order** Hemiptera
**Family** Cicadidae
**Body length** 23–55mm (1–2¼in)
**Distribution** Worldwide,
mainly warmer regions
**Number of species**
World–2500; NA–166; UK–1

BL.
(at rest)

**Identification** The species in this family are recognizable by
their distinctive shape and sounds. They are large and broad-
bodied with transparent and usually shiny, membranous
wings. Black, brown or green in general colour, they may have
dark markings or be cryptically patterned. The head is wide
and blunt-ended with large eyes and short antennae. The front
wings are larger than the hind wings and both may have bands
or spots of a dark colour. The veins do not reach the wing
margins. The front legs are larger than the others and have
strong teeth.
**Habitat** The nymphs are subterranean while the adults can
be found on shrubs and trees of various species.
**Biology** Cicadas are plant-feeders. The nymphs live on root
sap, sucking the fluid from xylem vessels. They moult many
times and because of the poor diet they can take anything from
4–17 years to reach adulthood. The nymphs are specially
adapted for digging, having strong, stout front legs. Cicadas
are easy to hear but very difficult to locate in their habitat. The
loud and species-specific songs are produced by a pair of
special organs known as tymbals located underneath the body
on the first abdominal segment. A stiff membrane, controlled
by a muscle, is rapidly clicked in and out, producing the
characteristic buzzing sound. In general it is the males who
sing and usually during the day, but both sexes have hearing
organs. A few species make sounds by vibrating their wings
together. Eggs are laid in the twigs of trees and shrubs. The
young nymphs drop, or fall with the damaged twig, to the
ground and burrow into the soil. The nymphs of the North
American species *Magicicada septemdecim* (the Periodic
Cicada) construct peculiar earth chimneys above ground in
which to complete their final moult. This species has races
which take 13 or 17 years to complete their life-cycle.
**Economic importance** Massive simultaneous emergences of
adults can result in huge numbers of eggs being laid in twigs of
perennial plants, trees and shrubs. Young trees may be killed
by losing large numbers of twigs or small branches.

# Leafhoppers

**Order** Hemiptera
**Family** Cicadellidae
**Body length** 3–20mm (¼–¾in), mostly under 15mm (⅝in)
**Distribution** Worldwide
**Number of species** World–21,000; NA–2700; UK–262

**Identification** Members of this massive family are green or brown in colour and may have brightly striped markings. They are more slender than froghoppers and are parallel-sided or taper towards the hind end. The head may appear broadly triangular or wide and blunt. All species can jump very well and the hind tibiae have one or two rows of small spines.
**Habitat** Very common everywhere; it is thought that virtually all plant species have at least one species of cicadellid.
**Biology** All cicadellids are herbivores, most species sucking the juices of plants' phloem vessels while some (Cicadellinae) feed on a poorer diet of xylem fluid. Females may lay up to 300 eggs in rows or clusters under the epidermis of their host plants. There may be four to six nymphal stages after which the young adults may migrate over quite long distances. In many species there can be several generations each year. When disturbed, cicadellids will jump and take flight rapidly. The nymphs produce large quantities of carbohydrate-rich excrement called honeydew. This waste can be expelled rapidly by some species (sharpshooters) or spotted onto the leaves. Ants and other insects find honeydew an irresistible food source. Parasitic and predatory wasps play an important part in controlling natural populations of these insects.
**Economic importance** Very many species are pests of cultivated plants, ornamentals and all manner of important crops, weakening them by their feeding and by acting as vectors for many viral and other diseases. *Circulifer tenellus* (Sugarbeet Leafhopper), *Empoasca fabae* (Potato Leafhopper) and *Typhlocyba rosae* (Rose Leafhopper) are typical examples. The attractive, candy-striped *Graphocephala fennahi* is found on blackberry and ornamental plants in North America and on rhododendron species in Britain and Europe.

*Graphocephala fennahi*

BL

# Treehoppers

**Order** Hemiptera
**Family** Membracidae
**Body length** 5–13mm (¼–½in)
**Distribution** Worldwide, mainly warmer regions
**Number of species** World–2500; NA–258; UK–2

**Identification** Members of this large family are green, brown
or black and can be easily recognized by the large and often
bizarrely shaped pronotum which extends backwards and
sideways to cover the abdomen. In tropical species, the
pronotal extension can assume incredible, branched or ant-like
forms. In most species the pronotum looks like a thorn, hump
or large spine under which the membranous wings are often
concealed. The head is blunt and sometimes dwarfed by the
size of the pronotum. The antennae are small, hair-like and
arise from below the compound eyes. The hind legs are
slightly enlarged, enabling these insects to make jumps over a
short distance.
**Habitat** Common on vegetation of all kinds, including shrubs
and trees, most membracid species are specific to one or a few
closely related host plants.
**Biology** All species are herbivores, the nymphs sucking the
sap of grasses, shrubs, trees and a huge variety of herbaceous
plants. Most species have one or two generations per year and
overwinter as eggs laid in plant tissue. The nymphs of many
treehoppers feed in aggregations and are attended by ants who
gather their sweet honeydew (liquid excrement) as food. The
treehoppers gain protection from their enemies by means of
this mutualistic relationship.
**Economic importance** Only a few species do damage to
economically important plants. The American Buffalo
Treehopper, *Stictocephala bisonia*, is now widespread in central
and southern areas of Europe. This species lays its eggs in the
twigs of apple and other fruit trees. The eggs are laid in slits in
the bark and the twig often dies beyond the injured site.

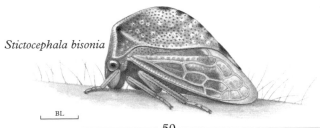

*Stictocephala bisonia*

BL

— 50 —

# Jumping Plant Lice

**Order** Hemiptera
**Family** Psyllidae
**Body length** 1.5–5mm (under ¼in)
**Distribution** Worldwide
**Number of species** World–1500; NA–260; UK–78

**Identification** These very small insects may look superficially like some small leafhoppers, but the antennae, which have ten segments, are much longer than those of any hoppers. Both sexes have two pairs of wings held together in a tent-like fashion over the body. The front wings are fairly tough with obvious veins and may be clear, clouded or with smoky patterns. The hind wings are much more delicate. Psyllids have their hind legs slightly enlarged and modified for jumping.
**Habitat** Found virtually everywhere, psyllid species are usually restricted to one or a few closely related host plants.
**Biology** Active insects, jumping and flying at the slightest disturbance, psyllids lay stalked eggs on plant surfaces or inside plants, where some may induce the formation of a gall. The nymphs, which are gregarious, distinctively flattened and with noticeable, developing wing pads, may pass through five stages before reaching maturity. In some species the nymphs produce white, waxy filaments as a protective device, while others are attended and protected by ants in return for sugar-rich honeydew.
**Economic importance** Some are important pests and are vectors of plant diseases. Of the many crops damaged, aubergines, tomatoes, potatoes and peppers are just a few. Transmitted viruses cause yellowing, reduction of yield, dwarfing and even death of affected plants. Two notable species are the Pear Sucker, *Psylla pyricola*, and the Apple Sucker, *P. mali*. Both species have been accidentally introduced to North America from Europe.

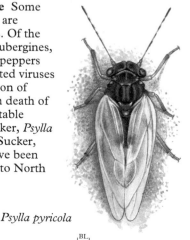

*Psylla pyricola*

BL

# Plant Lice, Greenflies or Aphids

**Order** Hemiptera
**Family** Aphididae
**Body length** 1–8mm (³⁄₈in),
mostly 5mm (¹⁄₄in)
**Distribution** Worldwide, mainly
northern hemisphere
**Number of species** World–2250;
NA–1350; UK–380

*Aphis fabae*

ws

**Identification** These familiar small,
soft-bodied insects are mostly green
but some are pink, black or brown.
The wings, when present, are held
tent-like over the body and may be
clear or with darkish markings. The
hind wings are much smaller than the
front wings. The end of the pear-
shaped abdomen has a short, pointed
tail and usually carries a pair of short
tubes, called cornicles, from which a defensive secretion
is produced.
**Habitat** Aphids occur on host plants of all kinds.
**Biology** Emerging spring aphids are all females and produce
large colonies by parthenogenetic reproduction. Most species
give birth to live nymphs (vivipary) and, as the season
progresses, more and more winged forms are produced, which
then migrate to a summer host plant. Feeding and
parthenogenetic reproduction continues. More winged forms
appear and return to the original host plant, where males and
females mate and lay eggs. Most species have two host plants,
one herbaceous, one woody. All species are plant-feeders,
taking in huge amounts of sap through their slender
mouthparts. Some species are gall-formers. Large quantities
of honeydew are produced and many species are attended by
ants. Interactions between ants and aphids can be complex.
**Economic importance** One of the most destructive of all
insect families, they have phenomenal reproductive powers
and are carried over long distances by wind. They damage
nearly all species of economically important plants. *Myzus
persicae*, the Peach-Potato Aphid, is a vector for 100 plant
viruses. *Aphis fabae* is the familiar garden blackfly. In North
America, some 80 species are pests of ornamental and crop
plants. Fortunately, large numbers of aphids are killed by
adverse weather and predacious insects.

# Whiteflies

**Order** Hemiptera
**Family** Aleyrodidae
**Body length** 1–3mm (less than ¼in)
**Distribution** Worldwide
**Number of species** World–1200; NA–100; UK–19

**Identification** Whitefly are very small and for most species, surprisingly, the adults are poorly known. Adults have two pairs of wings which are usually white but may be clear or clouded with spots or other markings. The hind and front wings are of the same size and are held horizontally over the body at rest. Whitefly can look like very small moths, but are, of course, completely unrelated. The nymphs are more commonly seen and are sedentary on the undersides of leaves. They are covered with a white, waxy secretion which they produce as a defensive strategy.
**Habitat** These tiny insects are common on their host plants in the wild or as pests in greenhouses or on house plants.
**Biology** First-stage nymphs are active, while later stages are sedentary. The nymphs moult four times before becoming adult and all stages suck phloem sap. The wings, unusually, develop on the inside, being everted during the moult of the final nymphal stage. The waxy covering of the nymphs is often species-specific and an aid to identification. Honeydew is excreted by all life stages and can cover leaves which may become blackened due to the growth of fungus (*Botrytis* spp.) on the honeydew.
**Economic importance** Many species have pest status. The well-known Greenhouse Whitefly, *Trialeurodes vaporariorum*, is cosmopolitan in distribution and infests the undersides of tomato and cucumber leaves. Other crops attacked by whitefly include citrus trees, grapes, avocado and strawberries. Biological control of the greenhouse whitefly can be effected by the use of a small, parasitic wasp, *Encarsia formosa*.

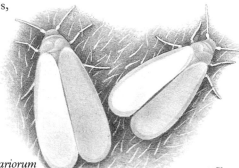

*Trialeurodes vaporariorum*

⊔ BL

# Mealybugs

**Order** Hemiptera
**Family** Pseudococcidae
**Body length** 1.5–8mm (less than ⅜in)
**Distribution** Worldwide
**Number of species** World–2000; NA–280; UK–35

**Identification** Unlike other families of scale insects, mealybugs have functional legs at all stages of their life history (in other, related families, there is a sedentary stage). The sexes are very different. Females are elongate, wingless, covered with a meal-like wax coating and have fully developed sucking mouthparts. The males look more like proper insects in having a pair of wings, but do not have developed mouthparts and do not feed. The bodies of these insects have strange pores through which the waxy covering is extruded.
**Habitat** Mealybugs are found on a variety of host plants. Most species are specific to a particular species of plant.
**Biology** All mealybug species are sap-suckers, infesting all parts of their host plants. The females of some species lay eggs, while others give birth to live nymphs. Temperate species have one generation per year, while those occurring in warmer regions may have five or six generations in a single year.
**Economic importance** Many species are injurious to crops and houseplants, and many are vectors for viral plant diseases. Among the crops attacked are coconut, pineapple, grape and sugarcane. *Planococcus citri* is a serious pest of citrus trees, coffee and avocado in hotter parts of the world, and is a general greenhouse pest in temperate regions.

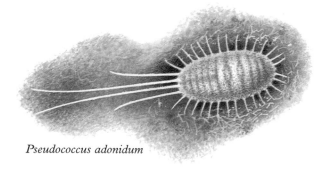

*Pseudococcus adonidum*

BL (exc. appendages)

# Soft, Wax and Tortoise Scales

**Order** Hemiptera
**Family** Coccidae
**Body length** 2–12mm (⅛–½in), mostly under 8mm (⅜in)
**Distribution** Worldwide, mainly tropical
**Number of species** World–1250; NA–92; UK–35

*Coccus hesperidum*

BL

**Identification** Members of this family show considerable variation in form, but in general female coccids are oval and flattened with a hard, smooth or waxy body. Wax-covered species appear white, while others may be brownish. The males, which are rarely encountered, may be winged or wingless, are short-lived and do not feed. The degree of development of the legs and antennae in these insects varies enormously but the females are almost always sedentary and do not look much like insects at all.

**Habitat** Coccids are usually found on their host plants in the wild, in greenhouses or on houseplants.

**Biology** All species are sap-suckers. Females reproduce mostly by parthenogenesis, the eggs being produced under their scale-like bodies. Many hundreds of eggs can be laid and the first-stage nymphs move away from their mother using their minute legs. This stage is the dispersal phase and the nymphs are called crawlers. The crawlers of some species have long terminal wax filaments which enable them to travel great distances on wind currents. The subsequent nymphal stages are sedentary and are stuck to the plant tissues by their slender mouthparts. The reproductive potential of these insects is immense.

**Economic importance** A large number of coccid species are important pests all over the world. Some species like *Coccus hesperidum* (the Brown Soft Scale) are pests of citrus trees and greenhouse crops, while other species attack ornamental plants and crops ranging from mango to spruce. Interestingly, some coccids produce large amounts of wax of such purity that it has been used for medicinal purposes and making candles.

# Bedbugs

*Cimex lectularius*

**Order** Hemiptera
**Family** Cimicidae
**Body length**
3–6mm ($\frac{1}{8}$–$\frac{1}{4}$in)
**Distribution**
Worldwide
**Number of species**
World–90; NA–14; UK–4

**Identification** These blood-sucking bugs are oval and flattened with vestigial wings. Generally reddish-brown in colour they may have a covering of silky pale hairs. The rostrum or beak lies in a groove on the underside of the body when not in use. The head is not very large. In some species, the rostrum is quite long.

**Habitat** Cimicids are found on their mammalian or avian hosts or in nests or crevices in buildings where their hosts are present.

**Biology** Unlike lice, bedbugs do not keep in permanent contact with their hosts. The adults and nymphs feed on blood at night, returning to their hiding places during the day. Fertilization is unusual, the males inject a sperm packet or spermatophore through the body wall of the females. This process is known as traumatic or intrahaemocoelic fecundation. The sperms migrate internally to the ovaries. In the case of the cosmopolitan Bedbug (*Cimex lectularius*) eggs are laid in crevices in floorboards and similar places. A female can lay up to 250 eggs during her lifetime and her eggs take anything from six weeks to six months to reach adulthood, depending on food supply. A blood meal is needed at each of the nymphal stages and, once adult, bedbugs can survive for long periods without food. These insects have bacteria in their guts which produce vitamin B, vital to life but lacking in their bloody diet. The genus *Cimex* contains species parasitic on man and poultry as well as other mammals and birds, while members of the genus *Oeciacus* attack swallows and martins. In North America another genus attacks condors.

**Economic importance** Bedbugs are common in cities where there are crowded or insanitary conditions. Human reactions to the bites vary greatly but usually there is an itchy red swelling around the area where the bug(s) fed. Like many other bugs, they have a distinctive odour which, once smelled, is never forgotten.

# Flower or Minute Pirate Bugs

**Order** Hemiptera
**Family** Anthocoridae
**Body length** 2–5mm ($\frac{1}{8}$–$\frac{1}{4}$in)
**Distribution** Worldwide
**Number of species** World–500; NA–85; UK–27

**Identification** These minute, flattened bugs can be elongate or oval in shape and are blackish or brownish with paler markings. The body may be shiny in appearance or dull, smooth or covered with fine hairs. Most species are fully-winged while others may be short-winged. The head appears pointed and the antennae have four segments. The piercing rostrum has three segments. The rear part of the front wings have no closed cells and few or no veins.

**Habitat** Anthocorids are often found in flowers but are present under bark, in vegetation, leaf litter and fungi. Some species live in mammal burrows, bird nests, bat caves, grain-stores and houses.

**Biology** These bugs are mainly predacious but some species will feed on pollen and other plant material. Adults and nymphs catch small insects and suck the juices from insects' eggs, larvae and pupae. Normally, females produce eggs but a few species have been shown to be viviparous. If handled, some species will attempt to pierce human skin which can be more painful than would be thought possible from such a small insect. Reproduction can be normal but very many species exhibit intrahaemocoelic or traumatic insemination.

**Economic importance** Anthocorid bugs are very useful in the natural control of insect populations. Their highly predatory habits have made them useful as biological control agents. Several species have been used to control aphids, thrips, scales and mites. *Orius, Anthocoris* and *Lyctocoris* are common genera. *Lyctocoris campestris* is widespread and can be found in grainstores where it may be of use in controlling pests. *Orius insidiosus* is an important predator of lepidopteran pests of corn in North America.

*Anthocoris confusus* ⌊BL⌋

# Damsel Bugs

**Order** Hemiptera
**Family** Nabidae
**Body length** 3–12mm (⅛–½in), mostly 7–11mm (⅜–½in)
**Distribution** Worldwide
**Number of species** World–400; NA–48; UK–13

**Identification** Nabids are usually dull brown or straw-coloured with a variety of indistinct spots and stripes. A few species may be black or other colours. The most distinctive feature is the four-segmented rostrum which is not pressed flat along the underside of the body. The rostrum is quite slender and held curved outwards from the body. The front femora of these relatively slender bugs are thickened and armed with short spines. The front legs are used to grip prey insects but they are not as strongly adapted for the purpose as the front legs of some Reduviidae. The antennae are thin and four or five-segmented. Many species have short- and fully-winged forms.
**Habitat** These insects are found on the ground and in vegetation of all kinds wherever there are small insects.
**Biology** Nabids are highly predacious, catching and sucking out the body contents of aphids, caterpillars and a wide range of soft-bodied insects. Females lay their eggs on plant stems and the hatched nymphs seek their first, very small meal right away. There are several nymphal stages before adulthood is reached. Reproduction is normal but some males inseminate directly into the body cavity of the females, as in the Cimicidae. If handled, nabids can give a painful bite. *Nabis*, *Nabicula* and *Stalia* are common genera.
**Economic importance** Nabids are of great value in the control of natural insect populations, many species eating potential pests.

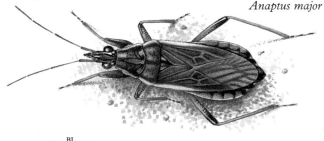

*Anaptus major*

BL

# Plant Bugs

**Order** Hemiptera
**Family** Miridae
**Body length** 1.5–15mm (⅛–⅝in)
**Distribution** Worldwide
**Number of species** World–7000; NA–1950; UK–210

*Lygus
rugulipennis*

BL

**Identification** Mirids can be variously coloured green, brown, red, black and with a great diversity of markings. They are relatively delicate, small, oval or elongate. The rostrum and the antennae have four segments and the hind part of the front wings has two closed cells. Most species are fully-winged, but short-winged or wingless forms occur.
**Habitat** Plant bugs can be found in every habitat, on vegetation of all types and from ground level to the tree tops.
**Biology** This family comprises the largest group of true bugs (Suborder: Heteroptera) in the world. The estimated total number, when the neotropical fauna is fully described, may be as high as 20,000. Diverse in all aspects of their biology, most are plant-feeders eating seed, fruit, leaves and all manner of plant juices. Others are predacious or partly predacious on aphids, mealybugs, scales, mites and many kinds of small, soft-bodied prey. Some species walk over the leaves of insectivorous plants where they feed on the plant's victims and some are able to feed on prey caught in spider webs. Other species can feed on carrion, dung, blood and honeydew. The eggs of mirids are laid inside plant tissues and overwinter before hatching in the spring. There are five nymphal stages.
**Economic importance** Many herbivorous species are pests. Species of the genus *Lygus* can do great damage to legumes, vegetables, flowers and other crops. *Lygus pabulinus* is a cosmopolitan pest species. *Leptopterna dolabrata* occurs in large numbers in meadows and can damage grasses. In tropical regions mirids can be pests of crops such as tea and coffee. Some mirids can be helpful as predators of pests.

# Lace Bugs

**Order** Hemiptera
**Family** Tingidae
**Body length** 2–5mm (⅛–¼in)
**Distribution** Worldwide
**Number of species** World–1820; NA–160; UK–23

**Identification** These small bugs are probably the most beautiful of all hemipterans, but a hand lens or binocular microscope is needed to appreciate the incredible lace-like or net-like patterns of reticulation on the dorsal surfaces. The pronotum and front wings may be elaborately sculpted, ridged and pitted. The pronotum is often extended like a hood over the head and to the sides and back towards the abdomen. Most species are greyish and somewhat rectangular in general appearance. The antennae and rostrum have four segments.

**Habitat** Tingids are found on the undersides of leaves or in flowers of herbaceous plants or in the foliage of trees and shrubs.

**Biology** All species are herbivorous, their feeding often causing yellow spots on leaves. Large numbers of these bugs may cause leaves to wither and drop. Tingid eggs are laid upright in plant tissue or near veins on the undersides of leaves. A liquid, injected at the time of oviposition, hardens to form a small raised bump on the leaf surface. The nymphs may be spiny but do not have the lace-like sculpturing of the adults. Most species feed in aggregations, some are attended by ants and a few are gall-formers. *Acalypta*, *Tingis* and *Dictyonota* are common genera.

**Economic importance**
Several species have pest status, including *Stephanitis pyri*, which attacks pear trees in Europe, and *Corythucha arcuata*, which can be injurious to oak, maple, apple and roses in North America. Tingids can be useful as weed control agents. *Teleonemia scrupulosa* has been introduced to parts of the world where its hosts, *Lantana* spp., have become serious weeds.

*Dictyonota fuliginosa*

BL

# Assassin and Thread-legged Bugs

**Order** Hemiptera
**Family** Reduviidae
**Body length** 7–40mm (³⁄₈–1⁵⁄₈in), mostly 10–15mm (³⁄₈–⁵⁄₈in)
**Distribution** Worldwide, mainly tropical
**Number of species** World–5500; NA–110; UK–6

**Identification** These bugs may be robust and oval or delicate and elongate with thread-like legs. In general, they are brownish, grey or blackish but some species may have bright red or orange markings. The head is elongate and has a transverse groove between the eyes. The antennae have four main segments and many subsegments. The three-segmented rostrum is distinctively short, stout and curved. When not in use, it fits into a groove on the underside of the front part of the body. The front legs are often thickened and used to grasp prey insects.
**Habitat** Reduviids are found on vegetation of all kinds.
**Biology** All these bugs are highly predacious or blood-sucking. In terrestrial ecosystems they form the main group of predatory bugs. Small species prey on mosquitoes and other small flies, while more robust species can attack quite large beetles. Many species mimic their prey in colour and shape. A few species suck the blood of birds and mammals. Reduviids can make sounds by scraping their rostrum along the ridged groove inside which it normally rests. Some species have spiny nymphs that stick bits of debris or the sucked-out bodies of their victims on their back as a disguise.
**Economic importance** The Masked Hunter, *Reduvius personatus*, is found in human habitations, where it feeds on bed bugs. It can also inflict painful bites if handled. Assassin bugs of the genus *Triatoma* are often called kissing bugs for they bite people at night, especially around the lips and face. Some triatomines are vectors of Chagas' disease. This disease, prevalent in Central and South America, is caused by a protozoan, *Trypanosoma cruzi*, and can affect humans and animals.

*Reduvius personatus*

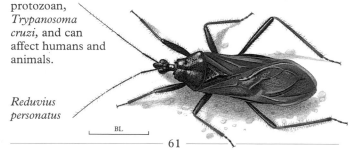

BL

# Shore Bugs

**Order** Hemiptera
**Family** Saldidae
**Body length** 3–7mm (⅛–⅜in)
**Distribution** Worldwide
**Number of species** World–300; NA–76; UK–22

**Identification** These small bugs are broadly oval, flattened, brown or black with pale markings. The eyes are very large and the rostrum is long. The antennae have four segments. The hind part of the front wings have four or five long, closed cells. The legs are relatively long and are adapted for jumping and rapid running.

**Habitat** Shore bugs, as their name implies, are found on mud around the margins of salt marshes, streams, ponds, ditches and similar places. Many species are found by the seashore among grasses, mosses and low vegetation. A few species, such as *Saldula orthochila*, live in dry habitats, but this is unusual.

**Biology** As far as is known, all saldids are predacious or feed on insect remains. They run, jump and fly rapidly and can burrow in mud, some species spending part of their life-cycle underground. They are difficult to catch as they hide in holes and rock crevices. Many can survive being submerged by the tide. *Salda* and *Saldula* are common genera.

**Economic importance** Saldids are of no significant importance.

*Saldula pallipes*  ⌐BL⌐

---

# Squash or Leaf-footed Bugs

**Order** Hemiptera
**Family** Coreidae
**Body length** 10–40mm (³⁄₈–1⁵⁄₈in), most under 20mm (³⁄₄in)
**Distribution** Worldwide, primarily tropical
**Number of species** World–2000; NA–120; UK–10

**Identification** Coreids are broadly oval bugs and most are dull brown with or without paler markings. Some exotic species may be yellow, red or shiny green. The abdomen of many species is flattened, projects laterally and is slightly raised. The head is usually much narrower and shorter than the pronotum. There are well-developed scent-gland openings on the thorax between the mid and hind legs. The males of some, particularly tropical, species have strong hind femora armed with spines and leaf-like expansions on the hind tibiae. The antennae are four-segmented and sometimes have leaf-like expansions.

**Habitat** These bugs can be found on their host plants in a variety of habitats.

**Biology** All coreids are herbivorous, eating shoots, fruits, buds and unripe seeds of their food plants. The common name is derived from the fact that many are attached to members of the plant family, Cucurbitaceae (squashes). The secretions from the defensive thoracic gland can be sprayed over a short distance by some of the larger species. The odour which is pungent and unpleasant or fruity is designed to protect the bugs from their enemies. There are no species common to North America and Europe.

**Economic importance** Several species attack crops such as asparagus, tomatoes, cotton, peaches, potatoes and oranges but they are not a significant problem in the northern hemisphere. One species, *Anasa tristis*, causes local damage to Cucurbitaceae in North America.

BL

*Coriomeris scabricornis*

63

# Broad-headed Bugs

**Order** Hemiptera
**Family** Alydidae
**Body length** 10–18mm (³⁄₈–³⁄₄in)
**Distribution** Worldwide
**Number of species** World–280; NA–29; UK–1

*Alydus calcaratus*

BL

**Identification** These slender, elongate bugs are very similar
in appearance to the Coreidae but their heads are broader and
nearly as long as the pronotum. Most species are yellowish-
brown or black and have an elongate body. The dorsal surface
of the abdomen may be brightly-coloured red and is only
exposed when the bug takes flight. The conspicuous openings
of the scent glands are located on the thorax between the mid
and hind legs. The antennae have four segments, the last
segment being slightly curved and longer than the third
segment. The legs of many species are spiny.
**Habitat** Alydids are common on roadside vegetation, in
wooded areas or in dry heathland.
**Biology** All species are apparently plant-feeders, particularly
on grasses and leguminous plants, although some have been
shown to be partly carnivorous, sucking the juices of carrion
and small insects. The nymphs of some alydids are very ant-
like and have been found in association with ants. Some adults
look like spider wasps presumably as a means of protection
through mimicry. The scent of these bugs is often stronger
than the smell produced by the Pentatomidae (stink bugs).
Some authors regard the Alydidae as a subfamily of the
Coreidae.
**Economic importance** There are no pest species in North
America or Europe but some species in the Oriental region can
damage rice crops.

# Scentless Plant Bugs

**Order** Hemiptera
**Family** Rhopalidae
**Body length** 5–14mm (¼–⅝in)
**Distribution** Worldwide
**Number of species** World–150; NA–36; UK–8

**Identification** Superficially similar to the Coreidae and Alydidae, these generally pale or light-coloured bugs differ in details of wing venation and in that they do not have obvious scent-gland openings on the thorax. The head is narrower than the pronotum and the antennae are four-segmented. A few species can be darkly coloured with reddish markings. These bugs can be heavily covered with punctures or tiny pits and may be very hairy. The surfaces of the head, pronotum and legs may have small tubercles or spines.
**Habitat** Rhopalids are most commonly found on weeds and other rank vegetation growing in old fields, by roadsides and in otherwise disturbed areas. There are a few tree-living species.
**Biology** All species are herbivorous, sucking the juices of ripe or unripe seeds, fruit and leaves of their host plants. Common in late summer and early autumn, *Liorhyssus* and *Stictopleurus* are genera typical of the northern hemisphere. *Liorhyssus hyalinus*, the Hyaline Grass Bug, varies in colour from black to pale yellow.
**Economic importance** A few species are crop pests.

*Liorhyssus hyalinus*   ⌊ BL ⌋

# Ground or Seed Bugs

**Order** Hemiptera
**Family** Lygaeidae
**Body length** 2–18mm (⅛–¾in), most under 12mm (½in)
**Distribution** Worldwide
**Number of species** World–3500; NA–300; UK–75

**Identification** There is a great deal of variation in size and colour between members of this large family. The majority are dull, pale yellow, brown and black while others can be bright red or orange with black, yellow or white markings in the form of spots or irregular bands. The body is elongate, oval, flattened and quite tough. The antennae arise from well down the sides of the head, below the eyes. Many of the ground-living species have short or wingless forms and some mimic ants. The front femora of some species are swollen and armed with stout spines.

**Habitat** Lygaeids are usually found close to the ground in leaf litter, under stones or on low-growing vegetation.

**Biology** The majority are seed-feeders, using the strong, toothed or spined front legs to grasp their food. Others are plant sap-suckers and a few are predacious. Ground-living species have well-developed scent glands to protect them from enemies. Sound production by stridulation may play an important part in the mating of these bugs. The genus *Nysius* is cosmopolitan. Species of *Drymus* and *Heterogaster* occur across the northern hemisphere.

**Economic importance**
One of the best-known pest species is the Chinch Bug, *Blissus leucopterus*, which does enormous damage to maize, wheat, rye, oats, barley and other grain crops in North America. Some lygaeids can be beneficial, like the broad-headed and large-eyed *Geocoris* species, which are predacious on aphids, scales, weevils, caterpillars and other pests. The milkweed seed-feeding species, *Oncopeltus fasciatus*, is used throughout the world as a laboratory and research insect.

*Kleidocerys resedae*

BL

# Stilt Bugs

**Order** Hemiptera
**Family** Berytidae
**Body length** 5–9mm (¼–⅜in)
**Distribution** Probably worldwide
**Number of species** World–180; NA–14; UK–9

**Identification** Most species in this family can be readily identified by their elongate, slender bodies and their very long, thin legs and antennae. Body colour varies from pale reddish- or yellowish-brown to grey. Some may look superficially like thread-legged reduviids but they do not have elongate heads or grasping front legs. The first segment of the four antennal segments is very long and swollen apically. The rostrum has four segments. The knees of these delicate bugs appear swollen.

**Habitat** Stilt bugs are found commonly among weeds and tall grass in woodlands, meadows and around the margins of ponds.

*Berytinus minor*

BL

**Biology** These bugs get their name from the way they walk with their bodies held high on spindly legs. The majority are fairly polyphagous herbivores but some species can be partly predacious, eating insect eggs and other small, soft-bodied prey. They are slow-moving and sometimes 'freeze' when disturbed. Eggs are laid on various plant parts. The nymphs are pale green or straw-coloured. In North America, there may be three or four generations per year. Species in the genera *Gampsocoris* and *Neides* look much more spindly and have relatively longer legs than species of *Berytinus* and *Cymus*. Because of their small size and secretive nature, they are often overlooked by the general collector.

**Economic importance** Stilt bugs are not damaging to crops and, as far as is known, are of no economic significance.

# Burrowing Bugs

**Order** Hemiptera
**Family** Cydnidae
**Body length** 2–10mm (⅛–⅜in)
**Distribution** Worldwide
**Number of species** World–400; NA–36; UK–9

**Identification** These broadly oval and slightly convex bugs look very similar to stink bugs but are smaller. They are generally shiny black or dark reddish-brown, often with blue tinges and white markings. The antennae are five-segmented. The sides of the pronotum are very often nearly straight. A distinctive feature is that the front tibiae are flattened and very spiny. The mid and hind tibiae are also very spiny.
**Habitat** Burrowing bugs can be found at ground level, under stones, dead leaves, decaying wood and around the base of various weedy herbaceous plants or similar low-growing vegetation.
**Biology** Nearly all the species in this family are phytophagous, and can burrow underground where the nymphs feed on root sap. Some species, such as those of the genus *Sehirus*, climb a little way up their host plants to feed. Some species have been shown to live in association with ants. Females of some species are known to guard their eggs.
**Economic importance** These bugs are of no known significance.

*Sehirus bicolor*

# Stink Bugs or Shield Bugs

**Order** Hemiptera
**Family** Pentatomidae
**Body length** 5–25mm (¼–1in)
**Distribution** Worldwide
**Number of species** World–5000; NA–250; UK–18

**Identification** Stink bugs are rounded, oval or shield-shaped. The predominant body colours are browns and greens but many can be very brightly coloured and conspicuously marked. The head is visible but can appear partly sunk into the pronotum in some species. The antennae have five segments. The pronotum is always broad and may have sharp points or angular corners. The tibiae are not spiny.

**Habitat** Pentatomids can be found on herbaceous vegetation, shrubs and trees in a wide range of habitats.

**Biology** The majority of stink bugs are primarily phytophagopus but many are carnivorous or mixed feeders. The barrel-shaped eggs are laid in small, regular clusters and the nymphs, which are flattened and rounded, are often differently coloured or patterned from the adults. These bugs produce very strong-smelling fluid from adult thoracic or nymphal abdominal glands. The fluids repel natural enemies, can stain human flesh and produce bad headaches in sensitive individuals. The defensive fluid is a mixture of volatile organic compounds and is often species-specific. *Picromerus bidens* feeds on both animal and plant tissue and was introduced to North America from Europe. *Zicrona caerulea* is an example of a predacious species. It feeds on beetles and caterpillars.

**Economic importance** Many herbivorous species are of considerable economic importance, particularly in tropical and subtropical regions of the world. *Nezara viridula* is almost cosmopolitan in distribution and can damage tomatoes, beans, cotton and other plants. *Murgantia histrionica*, the Harlequin Bug, is destructive to plants of the cabbage family. Predacious species are of value in controlling pests.

*Zicrona caerulea*

BL

# Water Striders or Pond Skaters

**Order** Hemiptera
**Family** Gerridae
**Body length** 2–19mm (⅛–¾in), mostly 10–15mm (⅜–⅝in)
**Distribution** Worldwide
**Number of species** World–500; NA–45; UK–9

**Identification** Gerrids are quite slender, dark brown or blackish and have a grey appearance due to a covering of very fine velvety hair. The rostrum is four-segmented. The front legs are short for grasping prey while the middle and hind legs are very elongate. The middle and hind legs arise very close together on the body and splay out to support the insect on the water's surface. The feet and underside of the body have a dense covering of water-repellant hairs. Most species have winged and wingless forms.
**Habitat** Water striders are the most commonly seen surface-dwelling water bugs and are present wherever there is still or slow-flowing water. Some species live on the oceans.
**Biology** These bugs are superbly adapted for catching small dead or drowning insects on the surface of water. Their unwettable legs support them and they can run across the surface film at surprising speeds. Ripple-sensitive hairs on their legs enable them to locate likely victims. *Gerris* is a cosmopolitan genus whose member species lay their eggs in a slime-covered mass attached to plants just below the surface. Other gerrids may lay their eggs on floating objects or on the surface of the water. *Gerris remigis* is a common North American species, while in Europe *G. lacustris* takes its place. Species of the genus *Halobates* are often called ocean striders and are the only truly marine insects.
**Economic importance** Of no significant importance.

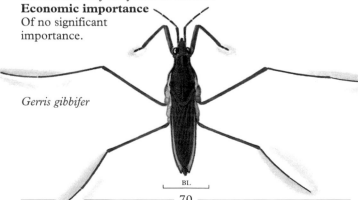

*Gerris gibbifer*

BL

# Water Measurers or Marsh Treaders

**Order** Hemiptera
**Family** Hydrometridae
**Body length** 7–15mm (³⁄₈–⁵⁄₈in)
**Distribution** Worldwide, primarily tropical
**Number of species** World–110; NA–9; UK–2

**Identification** The body, head and legs of these reddish to dark brown bugs are very slender and stick-like. The body is supported by the stilt-like legs and at first glance they may resemble very small stick insects. The eyes are fairly large and bulge out slightly from the sides of the head. The antennae are four or five-segmented and the rostrum has three segments. The majority of species are wingless but short-winged or fully-winged forms occur in some species.
**Habitat** Quiet pools, marshes, swamps and stagnant water are typical habitats for hydrometrids.
**Biology** The very long eggs of these bugs are laid singly and glued to objects or marginal vegetation. The nymphs and adults are very slow-moving and feed on small insects and other aquatic organisms. Small crustaceans such as water fleas may be skewered by the slender rostrum. *Hydrometra* is the commonest genus in North America and Europe.
**Economic importance** Hydrometrids are of no economic importance.

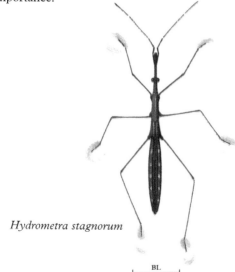

*Hydrometra stagnorum*

BL

# Backswimmers

**Order** Hemiptera
**Family** Notonectidae
**Body length** 2–17mm (⅛–⅝in)
**Distribution** Worldwide
**Number of species** World–300;
NA–35; UK–4

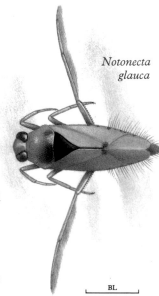

*Notonecta
glauca*

BL

**Identification** The dorsal body
surface of these stout, wedge-
shaped bugs is convex with a ridge
or keel running down the middle.
In general the head, pronotum and
front wings are pale-coloured with
dark markings. The wings may
have clear pale, oblique, broad
bands. The body beneath the
wings is dark brown to black. The
eyes are large, dark and shiny. The
ventral surface of the body is
normally dark brown or black.
The stout rostrum has three or four segments and the
antennae, which are short and hardly visible, have four
segments. The front two pairs of legs are short and used for
grasping food, while the clawless hind legs are long with
fringes of hairs and are used as oars. The body surface under
the wings has a covering of long hairs which allows air to pass
from the rear end of the bug to the spiracles on the thorax.
**Habitat** Backswimmers prefer still, open water in small pools,
streams and around the margins of lakes.
**Biology** These bugs are underwater predators and will feed
on insects, tadpoles, small fish and even fingers if given the
opportunity. Their common name derives from the fact that
they swim upside down and, when resting at the surface, will
hang from the end of their abdomen. In some countries, the
common name 'water boatmen' is applied to this family but
should really refer to the Corixidae. They are strong swimmers
but can leap into the air through the surface film and fly away.
Males can make sounds to attract females by rasping their
rostrum on the front legs. Some notonectids insert their eggs
into aquatic plant tissue while others simply glue their eggs to
the plants. Species of the genus *Notonecta* are common across
the northern hemisphere.
**Economic importance** These bugs are of no significant
importance but may bite people.

# Water Scorpions

**Order** Hemiptera
**Family** Nepidae
**Body length** 15–45mm ($\frac{5}{8}$–$1\frac{3}{4}$in)
**Distribution** Worldwide, primarily tropical
**Number of species** World–200; NA–13; UK–2

**Identification** These bugs are greyish-brown or reddish-brown in colour and may have bands of contrasting colour on the legs. They may be broadly oval, flattened with shortish legs or cylindrical, elongate with relatively long legs. In all species, the rostrum is short and stout and the front legs are strongly modified for catching prey (raptorial). The head is short and the eyes appear spherical. The mid and hind legs are used for walking and, in elongate species, arise close together on the body, well behind the front legs. The majority of species are fully-winged but rarely fly. Nepids have a posterior breathing tube which, in some, may be as long as the rest of the body.
**Habitat** These aquatic bugs can be found in slow-moving or still water. Some prefer the shallow water of muddy-bottomed ponds while others prefer deeper water.
**Biology** Nepids are slow-moving and highly predacious bugs which hide in vegetation to ambush their prey. Mosquito larvae, tadpoles and a variety of aquatic organisms may be seized and eaten. The long posterior breathing tube is made in two grooved halves joined by rows of hooked bristles and is thrust through the surface film, allowing the bugs to breathe. Species of the genus *Ranatra* are long and slender with a very long pronotum and elongate front legs. They are often called water stick insects. Species of *Nepa* are much flatter, broader and stouter with a normal pronotum and stouter front legs. Female nepids lay their eggs on submerged objects or inside the tissue of aquatic plants. Adults and nymphs can make sounds by rubbing the base of their legs against the body and many feign death.
**Economic importance** Of no significance but can give a painful bite if handled carelessly.

*Nepa cinerea*

BL

(inc. tail)

# Water Boatmen

*Glaenocorisa propinqua*

**Order** Hemiptera
**Family** Corixidae
**Body length**
3–15mm (⅛–⅝in)
**Distribution** Worldwide
**Number of species**
World–525;
NA–132; UK–34

BL

**Identification** These streamlined bugs are very similar in appearance to the Notonectidae but can be distinguished in the field because they rest horizontally under the surface and do not swim upside down. The dorsal body surface is flattened without a central keel and the middle legs are more or less the same length as the hind legs. They are dark reddish- or yellowish-brown often with fine transverse markings in the form of bands, mottling or other patterns. The under body is pale coloured. The head has large, dark eyes and a very short, stout rostrum. The front legs have scoop-shaped ends for feeding, the middle legs are used for holding vegetation and the clawless back legs are fringed with long hairs to provide propulsion.

**Habitat** Corixids can be found in the still and slow-flowing water of ponds, lakes and less commonly in streams. Some species can be found in brackish water above high tide mark.

**Biology** These bugs are unusual in that they feed on algae, diatoms and plant debris at the bottom of well-vegetated ponds using their hair-fringed front legs to filter through the debris. Some species are unique among the bugs as they eat small particles of solid food (all other bugs suck up liquid food). Other species are predacious on small insect larvae. They swim rapidly and in a seemingly haphazard manner but spend a lot of time clinging to submerged plants. Corixids carry bubbles of air under their wings where the concave, dorsal surface of the abdomen acts as a reservoir. Females attach their eggs to submerged objects using a sticky glue. Males can stridulate very loudly, rubbing their front legs on their heads during courtship. They fly well and are attracted to lights. There are many common genera such as *Sigara*, *Cenocorixa*, *Arctocorixa* and *Hesperocorixa*.

**Economic importance** Unlike most other aquatic bugs, corixids will not bite. In subtropical and tropical regions, some are so common that they have been eaten by humans.

# Predacious, Banded or Broad-winged Thrips

**Order** Thysanoptera
**Family** Aeolothripidae
**Body length** 1–2mm (⅛in)
**Distribution** Temperate regions
**Number of species** World–250; NA–57; UK–11

**Identification** As with all thrip families, members of this family are minute, dark, narrow-bodied insects with hair-fringed wings. The body of these thrips is not particularly flattened and the front wings are relatively broad, rounded at the ends and generally lie parallel to each other when folded. The wings may have cross bands or mottled patches. There are two longitudinal veins along the full length of the wings and there are several cross veins. The hind wings are slightly smaller than the front wings. Predacious thrips are generally yellowish-brown to dark brown in colour. The antennae have nine segments. The ovipositor is curved upwards. Some unusual species are nearly wingless and look very ant-like.

**Habitat** These thrips can be found on various parts of cruciferous and leguminous plants, grasses and conifers.

**Biology** Although most species are pollen-feeders, many species in this family are predacious, feeding on other thrips, aphids and other small insects and mites. The best known and commonest genus is *Aeolothrips*. *Aeolothrips fasciatus* has a very wide distribution, is yellow to dark brown with banded wings and is commonly found in the heads of clovers. The nymphs are yellow or orange. The fully developed nymphs form a silken cocoon underground before emerging as adults.

**Economic importance** A few aeolothripids are of use in controlling natural populations of mites and aphids.

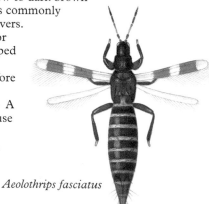

*Aeolothrips fasciatus*

Illustration made from slide-mount

⌐WS

# Common Thrips

**Order** Thysanoptera
**Family** Thripidae
**Body length** 0.7–2mm (⅛in)
**Distribution** Worldwide
**Number of species** World–1500; NA–265; UK–105

**Identification** The wings of these thrips are narrower than in the Aeolothripidiae and their ends are more pointed. The body appears flattened and the ovipositor in females bends downwards not upwards. The antennae have between six and nine segments. They vary from pale yellow through brown to black in colour. The wings seldom have tranverse bands of paler coloration.
**Habitat** Common thrips are to be found on the leaves and flowers of a vast range of plants.
**Biology** The vast majority of these thrips suck plant sap, others feed on fungal spores or are predacious. Adults of many species can be found in huge numbers in flowerheads although their nymphs may feed elsewhere. Common genera include *Thrips*, *Limothrips* and *Taeniothrips*.
**Economic importance** There are very many injurious species, some of which can do serious damage to a wide range of important crops. Among the many plants affected are peas, beans, citrus trees, cereals, coffee, tea, tobacco, onions, cultivated flowers and all manner of greenhouse produce. The Grain Thrips, *Limothrips cerealium*, is a widespread pest. It breeds in the ears of cereal crops and emerges in huge swarms when the crop is ripe. These tiny insects are often called thunder flies because of their association with this type of weather although the name is also used in the broader sense to cover all kinds of thrip.

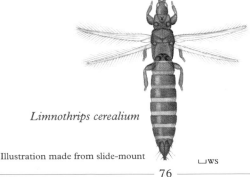

*Limnothrips cerealium*

Illustration made from slide-mount ⌐⌐WS

# Tube-tailed Thrips

**Order** Thysanoptera
**Family** Phlaeothripidae
**Body length**
1.5–4.5mm (⅛–¼in)
**Distribution** Worldwide
**Number of species** World–2700;
NA–348; UK–38

*Haplothrips
kurdjumovi*

⌐⌐ws

**Identification** The most
characteristic feature of this family is
that the end of the abdomen is tubular
and pointed. The species are in general
rather larger and stouter-bodied than
aeolothripids or thripids and the females do not have an
ovipositor. Most are dark brown or black but often have lighter
coloured and mottled wings. The antennae have eight
segments. A good recognition feature is that the wings, when
present, overlap each other when folded. The wings have no
veins or, in some, a single short vein. This family contains
some of the world's largest thrip species. A few tropical genera
such as *Phasmothrips* have species measuring up to 12mm
(½in) in length.
**Habitat** Tube-tailed thrips can be found on a wide range of
herbaceous plants, shrubs and trees, in flowers, on twigs and
under bark. Some are soil and leaf-litter dwellers.
**Biology** The majority of species feed on fungal threads and
about 400 species feed on the spores of fungi on twigs and
bark. Some 300 species worldwide induce and feed inside galls
on a range of host plants. Some genera have predacious
species which feed on mites and small, soft insects such as
whiteflies. *Haplothrips* contains predacious and herbivorous
species. The black *H. leucanthemi* is common in daisy flowers.
The immature stages are often brightly coloured red or yellow
and live in aggregations with the adults.
**Economic importance** Some species are pests while others
can be of benefit as predators of other small insects. *Liothrips
vaneeckei* damages the bulbs and other parts of lilies. Other
important plants affected include olives and grasses.

Illustration made from slide-mount

# Alderflies

**Order** Megaloptera
**Family** Sialidae
**Body length** 10–20mm (³/₈–³/₄in), most under 15mm (⁵/₈in)
**Distribution** Primarily northern hemisphere
**Number of species** World–75; NA–23; UK–2

**Identification** Alderflies are dull, dark brown to blackish-grey, stout-bodied insects often with pale or darkly tinted wings. At rest, the wings are held together, tent-like, over the body. The wing venation is fairly complex and is similar to snakeflies and lacewings. The pronotum is rather square and not elongate. The head is blunt, broadly square and the antennae are long and thread-like. The hind wings are broader at their base than the front wings and the veins of both pairs are not forked close to the wing margins. The ovipositor is not visible on the outside of the body.
**Habitat** These insects are found resting on alder and similar waterside vegetation.
**Biology** The adults are day-flying and spend much of their time resting. The larvae are aquatic and can be found under stones in muddy-bottomed ponds, canals and slow-moving streams. The larvae are highly predacious on all manner of small aquatic insects and worms and have large, powerful, sharply-toothed mandibles. The short-lived females lay eggs in regular masses, each containing several hundred eggs, on reeds, the leaves of marginal vegetation or stones very close to the water. When the young larvae hatch they crawl into the water on their well-developed legs. The larval abdomen has a single terminal gill and seven pairs of lateral gills, all of which have a feathery appearance. Pupation occurs in soil or moss and the pupae are capable of making their way to the surface in order that the adults can emerge freely. A common European species, *Sialis lutaria*, is very similar to many North American species. All the species in North America belong to the genus *Sialis*.
**Economic importance** Alderflies are of no significant economic importance.

*Sialis lutaria*

BL

# Snakeflies

**Order** Megaloptera
**Family** Raphidiidae
**Body length** 6–28mm (¼–1¼in)
**Distribution** Primarily northern hemisphere
**Number of species** World–85; NA–18; UK–4

*Raphidia xanthostigma*　　ws

**Identification** These moderately shiny, dark greyish or dark
reddish-brown insects are closely related to the alderflies but
differ in a number of characters, the most noticeable of which
is the elongated neck (the pronotum being much longer than
wide) on which the head can be raised. The head carries
moderately sized antennae, is broadest across the eyes and
tapers behind. The clear wings have similar complex venation
to that in alderflies but the veins are forked close to the wing
margins. Both pairs of wings have a small dark or pale mark
(the pterostigma) on the front edge towards the wing tips. The
females have a long, slender and easily visible ovipositor.
Females are a little larger than males.
**Habitat** Snakeflies can be found in wooded areas among rank
vegetation.
**Biology** Adults and larvae are highly predacious, feeding
largely on aphids and similar small, soft-bodied insects. The
eggs are laid into slits in bark. The long, slender larvae have
well-developed heads and legs, are completely terrestrial and
found under loose bark, in rotting wood or leaf litter. The
short, curved and pointed mandibles are similar to those of the
adults. The larval abdomen does not have any gills or
processes. The commonest genera are *Raphidia* and *Agulla*.
*Raphidia notata* is found in oak stumps while another common
species, *R. maculicollis,* is associated with coniferous trees.
**Economic importance** Snakeflies are of no significant
economic importance.

# Brown Lacewings

**Order** Neuroptera
**Family** Hemerobiidae
**Body length** 4–12mm (¼–½in)
**Distribution** Worldwide
**Number of species** World–900; NA–58; UK–29

*Micromus angulatus*

⌞ WS ⌟

**Identification** Hemerobiids are small to moderate-sized insects and are grey, brown or black in colour with clear or dusky wings. The wings are oval or less commonly narrow in shape and the hind wings are smaller than the front wings. The venation is complex and there are many forked veins at the wing margins. The wings of many species have mottled or speckled patterns of brown markings. The antennae are thread-like and may be as long as the front wing length.

**Habitat** Brown lacewings are common inhabitants of deciduous woodlands, gardens and hedgerows, and prefer low-growing vegetation.

**Biology** Members of this family are much less common than green or common lacewings. Both adults and larvae are highly predacious on mites and small, soft-bodied insects such as aphids, mealybugs and scales. The adults are usually active from dusk onwards and tend to hide in vegetation during the day. The eggs are laid on plants but are not supported by a slender stalk. The larvae are elongate, taper at both ends and do not have any body warts or tubercles. Larval body hairs are simple and not hooked. The mandibles of the larvae are short, stout and curved and are used to pierce prey. In its lifetime, a brown lacewing may eat many thousands of aphids. Widespread genera include *Hemerobius*, *Sympherobius* and *Kimminsia*.

**Economic importance** Brown lacewings are beneficial insects and are very effective in reducing natural populations of pests.

# Common or Green Lacewings

**Order** Neuroptera
**Family** Chrysopidae
**Body length** 10–25mm (³⁄₈–1in)
**Distribution** Worldwide except New Zealand
**Number of species** World–1600; NA–88; UK–14

**Identification** These insects are very similar to hemerobiids but are generally green in body and wing colour. The wings are iridescent with delicate tints of pink, green and blue. Some species are brown but the antennae of these lacewings are generally longer than those of the brown lacewings. The wing venation is complex with many veins forked at the wing margins. Good recognition features are the appearance of two seemingly zigzag veins in the outer half of the wings and the lack of dark patterning. The eyes are bright golden, brassy or reddish and seem to shine.

**Habitat** Green lacewings are very common and can be found in all types of vegetation where their prey lives.

**Biology** Both adults and their larvae are voracious predators of aphids, thrips, psyllids, scales, coccids and mites. In some species, the adults will eat pollen, nectar and honeydew. The adults are mainly nocturnal in habit and eggs are laid on vegetation, supported by long, delicate stalks. The larvae are stouter and broader than those of the brown lacewings, their backs have warts or tubercles bearing hooked hairs and the mandibles are more slender and curved. The larvae are pale yellow, white or greenish with brown or black markings and often disguise themselves by attaching the sucked-out bodies of their prey to the hooked hairs on their backs. Some species of aphid can produce a sticky substance from their abdominal cornicles which hardens in the hollow jaws of lacewing larvae. Adults will often hibernate in houses and are attracted to lights. *Chrysopa* is a very common and widespread genus.

**Economic importance** Green lacewings are of great benefit in that they eat vast numbers of aphids and other pest insects. *Chrysopa carnea* has been used as a biological control agent.

*Chrysopa carnea*

BL

81

# Antlions

**Order** Neuroptera
**Family** Myrmeleontidae
**Body length** 35–120mm(1⅜–4¾in)
**Distribution** Worldwide, mainly tropical or arid areas
**Number of species** World–1000; NA–80; UK–0

**Identification** These large, slender-bodied insects look like
damselflies but are softer and have short-knobbed or club-
ended antennae which are about as long as the head and
thorax combined. The body colour varies from yellow or green
to dark brown with darker markings. The wings are long and
narrow and may be clear or distinctively marked with brown or
black patterns. The head is much broader than the pronotum
and the eyes are large and conspicuous. The abdomen is long
and thin and, in males, bears sexual clasping organs that look
like the forceps of earwigs.
**Habitat** Open woodland, scrub grassland, dunes and warm,
dry sandy areas are typical habitats for antlions.
**Biology** Although some species eat pollen, most adult
antlions are carnivorous, seizing insects from vegetation. Most
are weak fliers and nocturnal in habit. Adults rest during the
day with their wings folded over the body. The females lay
single eggs in soil or sand. Some larvae construct insect-
trapping pits in loose sand, while others live on the trunks of
trees in soil or under stones and debris. All species are
carnivorous as larvae, preying on a wide range of insects and
spiders. In species of the genus *Myrmeleon*, the larvae live in
sand at the bottom of conical pits with only their jaws
showing. Ants or any other insect stumbling into the pit
tumble to the bottom or are showered with sand grains flicked
up by the antlion. Once at the bottom, the prey is sucked dry.
Antlion larvae, which are called doodlebugs in North America,
are broadly oval with very large jaws armed with sharp spinous
teeth. There are some 40 species of Myrmeleontidae in
southern Europe.
**Economic importance** Antlions are of no economic
significance.

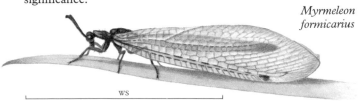

*Myrmeleon
formicarius*

WS

# Ground Beetles

**Order** Coleoptera
**Family** Carabidae
**Body length**
2–85mm (⅛–3⅜in),
mostly 4–25mm (¼–1in)
**Distribution** Worldwide
**Number of species**
World–25,000; NA–2270;
UK–330

*Calosoma*
*sycophanta*

BL

**Identification** A large
family of dull or shiny,
brown or black beetles
often with a metallic shine,
showing considerable
variation in size and shape. Some species have green, red or
white markings. The majority of species are flattened, parallel-
sided, dark and shiny, with grooves and punctures running
down the elytra. The head, thorax and abdomen of many
species appear very clearly differentiated from each other. The
legs are adapted for fast running, although in some species
they are modified for digging. The antennae join the head
between the eyes and the base of the jaws. In many species the
hind wings are reduced and the elytra are fused together.
**Habitat** These beetles are ground dwellers, living in a wide
range of habitats, under stones, wood and debris.
**Biology** Adults and larvae are predacious on small
invertebrates and carrion although some species are partly
herbivorous. The larvae are active hunters with well-developed
legs and powerful jaws. The majority of larvae are found in soil
and debris, are black or dark brown, elongate and taper
slightly at both ends. The adults of many species are nocturnal
while some are diurnal. Species of the genus *Calosoma* are
brilliantly coloured and hunt for caterpillars on trees and
shrubs. *Calosoma sycophanta* was introduced to North America
from Europe to control outbreaks of the Gypsy and Browntail
moths. The incredible bombardier beetles of the genus
*Brachinus* repel predators by blasts of hot, caustic quinones
fired with an audible pop from the end of their abdomens.
There are many genera common across the northern
hemisphere including, *Carabus*, *Nebria*, *Bembidion*, *Pterostichus*,
*Agonum* and *Harpalus*.
**Economic importance** Many species are beneficial in
controlling pest insects and some are destructive to snails.

# Tiger Beetles

**Order** Coleoptera
**Family** Cicindellidae
**Body length** 6–24mm (¼–1in)
**Distribution** Worldwide but primarily tropical
**Number of species** World–2000; NA–108; UK–6

**Identification** These beetles are very similar in basic design
to the ground beetles but differ in some features. The body is
elongate, slightly flattened and bears long, erect hairs. Tiger
beetles are usually very brilliantly coloured, metallic or
iridescent green, black or brown with patterns of various kinds.
The width of the head across the eyes is wider than the
pronotum. The eyes are very large and the antennae arise on
the head above the bases of the jaws which are large, curved
and sharply toothed. The legs are long and very spiny.
**Habitat** Tiger beetles are found running over the ground in
sunny, open areas.
**Biology** The name derives from the fact that these beetles are
very fierce predators and will catch and eat any insect or small
arthropod they encounter. Ants are a favourite food. Adult
tiger beetles are among the fastest insect runners. Most species
are good fliers and make a characteristic buzzing sound. The
larvae live in vertical burrows which they make in sandy soil.
The top of the head and the back of the thorax form a flat
cover for the burrow entrance and any passing insect is quickly
seized and dragged down to be eaten. To prevent them from
being pulled from their burrows by large prey, tiger beetle
larvae anchor themselves by means of special hooks on the
fifth abdominal segment. This family is sometimes treated as a
subfamily of the ground beetles. *Cicindela* is a common and
widespread genus.
**Economic importance** Undoubtedly efficient at killing
other insects, tiger beetles are of some value.

*Cicindela hybrida*

BL

# Diving Beetles

**Order** Coleoptera
**Family** Dytiscidae
**Body length** 2–34mm ($\frac{1}{8}$–1$\frac{3}{8}$in), mostly 5–25mm ($\frac{1}{4}$–1in)
**Distribution** Worldwide
**Number of species** World–3500; NA–475; UK–110

**Identification** Diving beetles are very streamlined and oval.
Both the top and undersides are convex, smooth and shiny.
The general body colour is black or dark brown but many
species have yellow, green or brown bands, spots and other
patterns. The head is partly sunk into the pronotum. The hind
legs are flattened with fringes of hairs and serve as paddles for
underwater propulsion. The front tarsi of males have peculiar
swollen, gripping structures which are used during mating to
hold the smooth backs of the females.
**Habitat** Diving beetles are found in streams, ditches, canals,
lakes and ponds, usually preferring shallower water. Some
species are found in brackish water.
**Biology** Adults and larvae are highly predacious on a wide
range of aquatic organisms ranging from other insects to
snails, tadpoles, frogs, newts and small fish. The adults can
remain submerged for long periods as they carry a supply of air
trapped below their elytra and periodically renew the supply by
coming to the surface where they hang from the end of their
abdomen. Although these beetles are highly modified for
aquatic life, nearly all can fly well and are attracted to lights at
night. Adults have defensive glands to protect them from
predacious fish. Eggs are usually laid singly in a slit, cut by the
female, in a water plant stem. The larvae are often called water
tigers and are elongate with well-developed legs and large,
curved jaws. Larvae mainly obtain air from the surface and
pupate in wet soil close to water. They will attack
prey much bigger than themselves, sucking the
body contents of their victims through
grooved mandibles after pumping in
digestive enzymes. *Dytiscus*, *Agabus*
and *Hydroporus* are common genera.
**Economic importance**
Diving beetles are of no
significant importance although
owners of ornamental ponds
may lose a lot of aquatic
livestock.

*Colymbetes fuscus*

BL

# Whirligig Beetles

**Order** Coleoptera
**Family** Gyrinidae
**Body length** 3–16mm (⅛–⅝in)
**Distribution** Worldwide
**Number of species** World–750;
NA–58; UK–12

*Gyrinus minutus*

**Identification** These oval and
streamlined beetles are generally
black and may have a bronze or
steel-blue sheen in some species. At
first glance, it may appear that they
possess only front legs, the middle
and hind legs being very short, flat,
paddle-like and without hair
fringes. The front legs are long and
used for grasping prey. The head

BL

bears short, stout antennae and the eyes are peculiar in being
divided into upper and lower portions. The upper part is used
for above-water vision, the lower for subsurface vision.
**Habitat** Gyrinids can be found in large numbers on the
surface of still or slow-moving water of ponds and streams.
**Biology** The common name of this group is derived from
their fast, jerky and circular swimming motions. Adults and
larvae are predators and scavengers. Adults aggregate in large
numbers on the water's surface, avoiding each other and
locating prey by means of their ripple-sensitive antennae. Eggs
are laid in groups on the undersides of the leaves of water
plants. The bottom-living larvae are very elongate, and have
ten pairs of feathery, abdominal gills and pointed, sucking
jaws. Pupation occurs inside a cocoon which is either attached
to submerged plants or contained in mud cells by the water
margin. Most species are diurnal and hibernate during the cold
winter months. When handled, adults produce a fruity odour
which has been likened to apples or pineapples. *Gyrinus* is a
common and widespread genus comprising the major part of
the North American and British fauna.
**Economic importance** Gyrinids are beneficial as a major
component of their diet is mosquito larvae.

# Carrion or Burying Beetles

**Order** Coleoptera
**Family** Silphidae
**Body length** 5–40mm (¼–1⅝in), mostly under 20mm (¾in)
**Distribution** Primarily northern hemisphere
**Number of species** World–250; NA–42; UK–21

**Identification** These beetles are generally slightly flattened, black or brown and often have yellow, red or orange markings in the form of irregular transverse bands or spots. The body surface may be dull or shiny and some have a roughened texture. The head bears convex eyes, strong, curved mandibles and short, club-ended antennae. In many species the elytra are broad at the back and shortened, exposing several abdominal segments, while in others the abdomen is completely covered. The legs of most species are strong and spiny.

**Habitat** Most species can be found on the ground close to carcasses, dung, rotting fungi or in damp shady woodlands.

**Biology** These beetles are carrion-feeders, scavengers or generalist carnivores. A few species eat decaying plant material. Burying beetles are very strong and two adults can move an animal as big as a rat to a good location for burying. They normally excavate beneath the corpse causing it to sink into the ground. The adults have a good sense of smell and are quickly attracted to a dead animal. Eggs are laid on the carcass or in underground galleries. In some species, the young larvae may be fed on regurgitated carrion. Fly larvae which develop on the carrion are also eaten. Well-known genera include *Nicrophorus* (sexton beetles) and *Silpha*. *Silpha atrata* preys on snails while some other species attack caterpillars.

**Economic importance** Very important in nutrient recycling and carcass disposal. A few species are minor pests of some root crops.

*Nicrophorus vespilloides*

BL

# Rove Beetles

**Order** Coleoptera
**Family** Staphylinidae
**Body length** 1–40mm (⅛–1⅝in), mostly under 18mm (¾in)
**Distribution** Worldwide
**Number of species** World–27,000; NA–3200; UK–825

**Identification** This family is a very large and diverse group of smooth, black or brown, very elongate, parallel-sided beetles. Some species may have red, white or metallic markings, highly textured surfaces or be covered with hairs. The characteristic feature of the family is the very short elytra which expose five or six of the abdominal segments. The jaws are long, sharp and cross each other in front of the head. The antennae are short and thread-like or have clubbed ends.
**Habitat** Species can be found in a wide range of habitats. Larger species can be found on carrion, in the ground, in fungi, under stones, leaf litter, in decaying plant material, by ponds and streams, and in ants' nests.
**Biology** Rove beetles can be predators, scavengers or herbivores. The hind wings are relatively large and folded intricately under the short elytra. The abdomen is used to assist in hind wing folding. Most species can fly well, smaller ones being diurnal, larger species usually being nocturnal in habits. Some 300 species are associated with ants, preying on disabled or dead individuals and showing a strong mimetic resemblance to their hosts. They avoid attack by providing the ants with sweet secretions. A few species live in the fur of mammals where they prey on fleas and ticks. There are very many common and widespread genera, *Staphylinus*, *Tachyporus*, *Aleochara*, *Philonthus*, *Tachinus* and *Quedius* are a few. *Staphylinus olens* is the Devil's Coach Horse Beetle, which shows a typical defensive posture; the abdomen and head are raised and the jaws are opened wide.
**Economic importance** Vital components of terrestrial ecosystems.

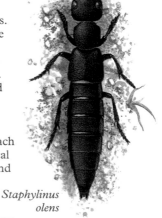

*Staphylinus
olens*

BL

# Stag Beetles

**Order** Coleoptera
**Family** Lucanidae
**Body length** 6–85mm (¼–3¼in), mostly 15–45mm
(⅝–1¾in)
**Distribution** Worldwide
**Number of species** World–1250; NA–32; UK–3

**Identification** Stag beetles are large, shiny, robust insects
with black or reddish-brown coloration. The large males of
most species have greatly enlarged and toothed mandibles,
whereas those of the female are much smaller. In some species
there are projections or horns on the head. The antennae are
elbowed with a terminal club of three or four flattened and
expanded segments. The elytra are smooth and shiny.
**Habitat** These beetles can be found in wooded areas, at lights
at night or along sandy beaches.
**Biology** The adult beetles may feed on plant sap and other
liquids while the larvae feed on decaying tree stumps and logs
in deciduous woodlands. Larvae can take many years to
complete development. They pupate inside a cell constructed
of masticated wood. The common name refers to the huge
male jaws, used for fighting during courtship. The jaws are
designed to fit round the edges of the rival's pronotum and
enable the beetles to flip each other upside down. Species of
the genus *Sinodendron* do not have enlarged male mandibles
and have small and cylindrical bodies. The best-known genus
is *Lucanus*, and although there are no holarctic species,
*L. elaphus* (NA) is very similar to *L. cervus* (UK).
**Economic importance** Lucanids are of no significant
economic importance.

*Lucanus cervus*

BL

# Earth-boring Dung Beetles

**Order** Coleoptera
**Family** Geotrupidae
**Body length** 5–42mm (¼–1⅝in), mostly under 25mm (1in)
**Distribution** Worldwide except New Zealand
**Number of species** World–550; NA–51; UK–8

**Identification** These stoutly-built beetles are broadly oval
and convex dorsally. They are shiny, brown or black and often
have a beautiful metallic blue or purple lustre. The head and
thorax of males often have tooth-like projections. The jaws are
large and clearly visible and the club-ended antennae have 11
segments. The elytra have longitudinal grooves or striations.
The tibiae of the front legs are modified for digging, being
broad and armed with strong teeth.
**Habitat** Geotrupids are found beneath dung of all kinds,
carrion and in decaying wood or fungi.
**Biology** Some authors treat this family as a subfamily of the
Scarabaeidae. Adults dig burrows many centimetres deep
below dung and carry it down to provide food for their white,
grub-like larvae. Tunnels are stocked with small balls of dung
and a single egg is laid in each one. Adults and larvae can
make noises by rubbing the bases of their legs on the body.
Some species are known to feed on plant material. The genus
*Geotrupes* contains many common and widespread species.
**Economic importance** Valuable as scavengers and dung
removers, most species are beneficial. Some plant-eating
species may be minor pests.

BL

*Geotrupes stercorarius*

# Scarab Beetles and their relatives

**Order** Coleoptera
**Family** Scarabaeidae
**Body length**
2–150mm (⅛–6in),
mostly under
40mm (1⅝in)
**Distribution** Worldwide
**Number of species**
World–20,000;
NA–1400; UK–89

*Serrica brunnea*

BL

**Identification** The family
is a very large and diverse
group of heavy-bodied,
dorsally-convex beetles. There is enormous variation in shape
and size between species. Body colour varies from dull browns
and black through red, yellow and orange to metallic blues and
greens. Despite this variation, a single character can identify
these beetles; the antennae have 8–10 segments and a
distinctive apical club made up of between three and seven
flat, expanded, moveable plates. The elytra do not usually
cover the abdomen completely. Unlike the Lucanidae, male
mandibles are not very enlarged.
**Habitat** These beetles can be found on dung, carrion,
decaying organic material of all kinds, fungi, flowers,
vegetation, under bark, in burrows and nests of vertebrates,
ants and termites. Even this list is far from exhaustive.
**Biology** The family is divided into many important
subfamilies which include the dung beetles, cockchafers, skin
beetles, rose chafers, rhinoceros and hercules beetles. The
larvae are typical white grubs with well-developed jaws and
many live in the soil, feeding on roots. Adults of many species
feed on pollen, nectar and other plant material. The dung
beetles, including the sacred scarabs of the ancient Egyptians
(subfamily: Scarabaeinae), roll dung with their hind legs and
lay one egg inside each ball. The goliath beetles of Africa are
among the largest of all insects, being 150mm (6in). Species of
the subfamily Melolonthinae are nocturnal and largely
herbivorous. *Aphodius*, *Serica*, *Onthophagus* and *Phyllophaga*
are among the genera occurring in the northern hemisphere.
**Economic importance** Many species are serious pests and
can do great damage to a large variety of fruit, vegetable, grain
and root crops, trees, garden and ornamental plants and
lawns. Dung-burying species are vital nutrient recyclers.

# Jewel Beetles

*Melanophila
acuminata*

**Order** Coleoptera
**Family** Buprestidae
**Body length** 2–65mm (⅛–2½in),
mostly under 30mm (1¼in)
**Distribution** Worldwide,
primarily tropical
**Number of species** World–14,000;
NA–675; UK–12

└ BL ┘

**Identification** Jewel beetles are among
the most beautiful of all insects. The vast majority are brilliant
metallic green, blue and red with very attractive markings in
the form of stripes, bands and spots. A few are dull brown or
black. They are tough-bodied, slightly flattened and taper
towards the hind end. The head is bent down and often
appears partly sunk into the pronotum. Their eyes are large
and their antennae are short, serrated or thread-like. The
surface of the body is very often sculptured with pits and
striations, and may be smooth, slightly hairy in parts or have
coloured scales.
**Habitat** Buprestids are typically inhabitants of coniferous and
deciduous woods. In the tropics, where they are much more
common, they live in hot, humid forests.
**Biology** Eggs are laid in wood. The white larvae are
distinctive with very small heads sunk into a very broad,
expanded prothorax. The rest of the body tapers towards the
back. Their antennae are short and the legs are extremely short
or absent. Because of their clubbed shape, the larvae are often
called flat head borers. They chew tunnels with an oval cross-
section in the roots and trunks of trees. Some species are leaf-
miners or bore in the stems of herbaceous plants or shrubs.
The adults mainly feed on nectar or foliage but a few species
are associated with fungi. Adults fly very rapidly in sunshine
and are difficult to catch. Some species do not open their
elytra when they fly, the hind wings being pushed out from
beneath. At the least disturbance jewel beetles will take to
flight or feign death. The genera *Melanophila*, *Anthaxia* and
*Agrilus* are common across the northern hemisphere.
**Economic importance** Many species are serious pests of
commercial, forest and orchard trees. Larvae are transported
around the world in timber and, as some take many years to
reach maturity, there have been cases of adults emerging from
furniture. The wing cases and other parts have been used in
embroidery and as jewellery in many parts of the world.

# Click Beetles or Skip Jacks

**Order** Coleoptera
**Family** Elateridae
**Body length** 2–60mm (⅛–2⅜in), mostly 10–30mm
(¾–1¼in)
**Distribution** Worldwide
**Number of species** World–8500; NA–890; UK–65

**Identification** The most recognizable feature of these mainly
brown or black beetles is their ability to click loudly and throw
themselves into the air when lying on their backs. Their bodies
are elongate, flattened and parallel-sided. The hind angles of
the pronotum are sharp and often extend backwards, forming
an acute point. The shoulders of the elytra are rounded. Some
species have eyespots on the pronotum or yellow, red or white
markings elsewhere on the body. Most species are slightly
shiny and smooth while others have coverings of short reddish-
brown or black hair. The antennae often have a comb-like
appearance.
**Habitat** Click beetles can be found on the ground under
litter, under bark, in decaying wood and on foliage of all kinds.
**Biology** The amazing jumping ability comes from powerful
thoracic muscles, a unique, loose jointing between the
segments of the thorax and a peg and groove catch. The power
of the jump, which is developed in about 0.75 of a millisecond,
forces the body against the ground and propels the beetle
upwards at up to 300 times the acceleration of gravity. The
larvae are cylindrical, elongate and tough-bodied and, as a
result, are called wireworms. They are carnivores, herbivores
and scavengers and are commonly found in rotten wood and
under bark or soil. *Ampedus,*
*Agriotes* and *Athous* are common
genera across the northern
hemisphere.
**Economic importance** Many
species have root-feeding larvae
which are destructive to beans,
potatoes, cotton, pasture plants
and a wide range of cereal and
root crops.

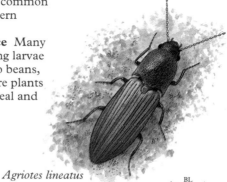

*Agriotes lineatus*

BL

# Soldier Beetles

**Order** Coleoptera
**Family** Cantharidae
**Body length** 3–30mm (⅛–1¼in)
**Distribution** Worldwide
**Number of species** World–4000; NA–468; UK–41

**Identification** Soldier beetles are black, brown or yellow with some parts of the body marked in bright yellow, red or orange. They are elongate, nearly parallel-sided and soft-bodied. The pronotum is relatively short and squarish. The elytra of some species are short, leaving just the very end of the abdomen exposed.
**Habitat** These colourful beetles can be found flying in warm sunshine and are common on flowers and vegetation in hedgerows, grassy areas and the edges of woodlands.
**Biology** The common family name comes from the resemblance of their colouring to old military uniforms. Both adults and larvae are predatory on other insects but the adults of some species eat the pollen and nectar of flowers such as milkweed, golden rod and wild parsley. The larvae are similar in general appearance to the larvae of ground beetles and are flattened, with a velvet covering of short hairs. They hunt for prey on the ground or in soil and very low-growing plants and mosses. Species of *Cantharis*, *Rhagonycha*, *Malthodes* and *Malthinus* are typical of the northern hemisphere.
**Economic importance** Cantharids are of no significant importance although they may be non-specific predators of pest insect species.

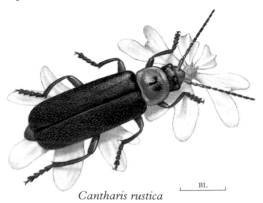

BL

*Cantharis rustica*

# Skin, Larder and Museum Beetles

**Order**  Coleoptera
**Family**  Dermestidae
**Body length**  1–12mm (⅛–½in)
**Distribution**  Worldwide
**Number of species**  World–800; NA–130; UK–16

**Identification**  Members of this family are dull brown or black, elongate or convex and broadly oval. They are often thickly covered with patterns of white, yellow, brown or red scales or hairs. The head is difficult to see as it is concealed by the pronotum. The front margin of the pronotum is much narrower than the hind margin. The short, club-ended antennae can be concealed in grooves on the underside of the thorax.

**Habitat**  Dermestids can be found in a huge variety of indoor and field habitats.

**Biology**  These beetles are incredible scavengers. The larvae feed on an enormous range of organic materials. Some adults feed on pollen. Eggs are laid in a suitable location on the preferred foodstuff and the very hairy larvae ('woolly bears') feed voraciously. Many species of *Dermestes* (larder, hide and bacon beetles) are cosmopolitan, and all the species in this genus feed on dried meat, carrion and all kinds of stored products. Species of the genus *Attagenus* (Black Carpet, wardrobe and fur beetles) eat carpets, fur, spices and dried milk. *Anthrenus* species (Variegated Carpet and Museum beetles) are mostly cosmopolitan and can be found in nearly all habitations, including museums where they can totally destroy collections of insects and anything else of an organic nature. The larvae of many species have long tufts of hairs which can produce nettle-rash.

**Economic importance**
Very many species are serious and often cosmopolitan pests in houses, shops, granaries and food stores, attacking foods, textiles, furs and important organic materials of all kinds. Some species of *Dermestes* have been used in the preparation of osteological material. The Khapra Beetle, *Trogoderma granarium*, is a serious cereal pest.

*Anthrenus verbasci*

⌐BL

# Furniture and Drugstore Beetles

**Order** Coleoptera
**Family** Anobiidae
**Body length** 1–8mm (⅛–⅜in), mostly 2–6mm (⅛–¼in)
**Distribution** Worldwide, mainly temperate regions
**Number of species** World–1500; NA–300; UK–28

**Identification** These small, hairy, light brown to black beetles will be better known to many people as woodworm, the name given to the larvae of the wood-boring species. Anobiid beetles vary in shape from elongate and cylindrical to broad and oval. The head is often hooded over by the pronotum and the antennae can have between 8 and 11 segments, with the last three segments lengthened or expanded. The legs are short and can be drawn in, fitting into special grooves.

**Habitat** Anobiids can be found in all types of wooden structure inside or outside and in stored plant products in shops, museum herbaria and human habitations.

**Biology** The eggs are laid on or in a suitable food source, which, in the majority of cases, will be dry wood. The larvae are soft and white with very small legs, and bore into the wood making small circular tunnels as they go. When fully grown they pupate just below the surface and emerge through the familiar small, circular holes. *Lasioderma serricorne* is the cosmopolitan Cigarette Beetle which attacks stored tobacco, spices and drugs. This species can complete its entire life-cycle on pure chilli powder and pepper. The Drugstore Beetle, *Stegobium paniceum*, is also cosmopolitan, the larvae feeding on a wide range of organic materials, including biscuits, bread, flour and drugs (it is particularly fond of opiates). *Anobium punctatum* is the much-dreaded Furniture Beetle whose larvae can destroy wood and wooden artefacts of all kinds. The Deathwatch Beetle, *Xestobium rufovillosum*, gets its name from the sexual signals that the beetles make in late spring. They prefer hardwood timbers and the adults tap their heads against the walls of their tunnels to attract mates. The faint sounds can be heard in a still room or church where a wake is being held.

**Economic importance** Many species are very serious pests of wood and stored products.

*Anobium punctatum*

BL

# Chequered Beetles

**Order** Coleoptera
**Family** Cleridae
**Body length** 2–30mm (1/8–1 1/4in), mostly 5–15mm (1/4–5/8in)
**Distribution** Worldwide, mainly tropical
**Number of species** World–3500; NA–270; UK–10

*Necrobia rufipes*

BL

**Identification** The majority of clerids are elongate, slightly flattened, soft-bodied and very hairy beetles with bright blue, green, red, brown or pink colouring. A few species are cryptically coloured, brown or black. The large head and dense body hair are usually sufficient to recognize these beetles. The antennae can be clubbed, toothed or comb-like.
**Habitat** Clerids are common on the foliage of woody plants and in wooded areas. Some species are found in association with stored animal products or carrion.
**Biology** The adults and larvae of most species are predacious although some adults feed on pollen and nectar at flowers. Clerid larvae are slender and cylindrical, can be brightly coloured blue, pink and orange and feed to a large degree on the larvae of bark beetles and other wood or bark-boring Coleoptera. Some species use the sexual pheromones of the bark beetle to locate their prey. Some larvae prey on the larvae of bees, wasps or on the egg pods of some grasshoppers. Species of *Opilio*, *Trichodes* and *Necrobia* are widespread and common.
**Economic importance** The attractive, metallic blue *Necrobia rufipes* (the Redlegged Ham Beetle) has a cosmopolitan distribution and, along with a few other species in the genus, is destructive to stored meat and meat products. The larvae will also eat the skin, bones and any other insect grubs (including each other). Bark beetle-feeding species are beneficial.

# Pollen or Sap Beetles

**Order** Coleoptera
**Family** Nitidulidae
**Body length** 1–14mm (¹/₈–⁵/₈in), mostly 2–7mm (¹/₈–³/₈in)
**Distribution** Worldwide
**Number of species** World–2800; NA–185; UK–95

**Identification** These small beetles are nearly always oval, squarish or rectangular in outline. The majority are brown or black and are often marked with reddish or yellowish irregular spots. In some species the elytra are a little shorter than the abdomen, exposing the last couple of segments. The antennae are shortish with very characteristic swollen or clubbed ends. The short legs are often wide and flattened.

**Habitat** Nitidulids can be found at flowers, fungi, tree wounds where sap is oozing, fermenting liquids, decaying fruits, carrion and other decaying animal matter. A few species are associated with the nests of ants and bees.

**Biology** Most adults and larvae feed on plant sap, nectar and pollen but a few are predacious on scale insects and others feed inside the seeds pods of plants. The larvae are white and cylindrical with well-developed legs and have similar habits to the adults. The genera *Meligethes*, *Carpophilus*, *Epuraea* and *Glischrochilus* have many common and widespread species.

**Economic importance** Anybody who wears yellow clothes in the summer will know just how annoying and common some nitidulids can be. They can ruin picnics and seem to be attracted in large numbers to bright, fresh paintwork. More seriously, some species of the genus *Carpophilus* can be pests of corn, dried and live fruit in orchards. A few *Meligethes* species can damage cruciferous crops like oilseed rape.

*Meligethes aeneus* BL

# Pleasing Fungus Beetles

**Order** Coleoptera
**Family** Erotylidae
**Body length** 3–25mm (⅛–1in), most under 15mm ⅝in)
**Distribution** Worldwide
**Number of species** World–2000; NA–65; UK–7

**Identification** In many species the head, pronotum and legs are reddish or reddish-brown and the elytra are black, green, or blue with a metallic sheen. Some species have distinct but irregular red or orange spots on the elytra. Erotylids are small to medium sized, slightly elongate to broadly oval and shiny. The antennae have 11 segments, the terminal three segments forming a stout club.
**Habitat** These beetles can be found around sap flows, fungi and rotting wood.
**Biology** The pale, elongate larvae have spiny plates on their bodies and well-developed legs. Most species feed inside the fruiting bodies of larger fungi or fungus-infected, decaying wood and stored produce. Species of the genus *Triplax* are commonly associated with bracket fungi such as *Polyporus*. Species of *Dacne*, *Tritoma* and *Triplax* are found across the northern hemisphere.
**Economic importance** A few erotylids are of minor economic importance.

*Dacne bipustulata* BL

# Ladybirds or Ladybugs

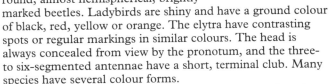

**Order** Coleoptera
**Family** Coccinellidae
**Body length** 1–10mm (⅛–⅝in)
**Distribution** Worldwide
**Number of species** World–5000;
NA–400; UK–41

*Adalia bipunctata*

BL

**Identification** Everyone will immediately recognize these oval or round, almost hemispherical, brightly marked beetles. Ladybirds are shiny and have a ground colour of black, red, yellow or orange. The elytra have contrasting spots or regular markings in similar colours. The head is always concealed from view by the pronotum, and the three- to six-segmented antennae have a short, terminal club. Many species have several colour forms.

**Habitat** Ladybirds are found virtually everywhere there is a good supply of their prey.

**Biology** The vast majority of these beetles, both adults and larvae, are highly predacious on soft-bodied insects. There are, however, some herbivorous species (*Epilachna*) which can sometimes be a pest on plants of importance such as beans and squashes. The predacious species are particularly fond of aphids and can consume vast quantities of these and other serious pests in the course of their life-cycle. The larvae are very active with well-developed legs and seek out colonies of aphids on their host plants. The soft-bodied larvae are often warty or spiny, have dark bodies with red or white spots, and, after moulting four times, they pupate on foliage. In some species, the larvae have body hairs which break easily to release a repellant liquid. Adult ladybirds show a phenomenon known as reflex bleeding. Toxic body fluids are produced at joints, especially the knees, and serve to deter would-be predators. The adults of many species hibernate in sheltered microhabitats and are often found in attics and cooler areas inside houses. Species of *Adalia*, *Coccinella* and *Pullus* are widespread and common.

**Economic importance** Of all the insect families (with the exception of the Apidae), this one is probably the most beneficial to man. Ladybirds are vitally important in controlling the natural populations of many pest insects and several species have been used as biological control agents. *Rodolia cardinalis* has been used for many years in the control of the citrus pest Cottony Cushion Scale.

# Darkling Beetles

**Order** Coleoptera
**Family** Tenebrionidae
**Body length** 2–45mm (⅛–1¾in), most under 20mm (¾in)
**Distribution** Worldwide
**Number of species** World–15,000; NA–1008; UK–37

**Identification** Darkling beetles are mostly black or very dark brown but some species can be pale brown or yellowish. The family is a very large one and there is enormous variation in shape and size between species. Some species look like ground beetles but they are not as shiny. Body shapes range from small, parallel-sided and blunt-ended to large and broadly oval. The antennae usually have 11 segments and can be relatively long and thread-like or short with clubbed ends. The eyes are often notched but not circular or oval in outline. The surface of the body may be smooth and shiny or dull and roughened and the pronotum in some species may have forward-pointing projections. Many species have very reduced hind wings and fused elytra.
**Habitat** Tenebrionids can be found in virtually all terrestrial habitats. Many species are adapted to life in very dry conditions such as in deserts and grainstores.
**Biology** These beetles are typical scavenging insects, eating a huge range of organic materials such as decaying vegetation, fungi, seeds, plant roots, the larvae of other insects and many stored products. The larvae are elongate, cylindrical, usually with very tough bodies and short legs. Desert tenebrionids have long legs and are able to collect moisture in the morning as dew condenses on their bodies. Some species are able to produce noxious chemical sprays to deter enemies.
**Economic importance** Many species, such as those of the genus *Tenebrio,* are pests in grain stores and similar places. *Tenebrio molitor* (the larva is called the yellow mealworm) is cosmopolitan. Species of *Tribolium* are called flour beetles and are pests of flour, cereals, dried fruit and meal of all kinds.

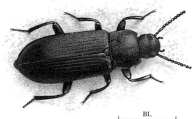

*Tenebrio obscurus*

BL

# Tumbling Flower Beetles

**Order** Coleoptera
**Family** Mordellidae
**Body length** 2–15mm (⅛–⅝in), mostly 3–9mm (⅛–⅜in)
**Distribution** Worldwide, mainly tropical
**Number of species** World–1250; NA–207; UK–10

**Identification** Mordellids have a very characteristic shape, being broad at the front, narrowing towards the hind end and appearing humpbacked in side view. The head is strongly bent downwards and the abdomen sticks out beyond the end of the elytra. Most species are brown or black in general colour and appear mottled grey on account of a dense covering of short, white, red or yellowish hairs or scales. The hind legs are often much longer than the other legs and the hind femora are expanded.

**Habitat** These beetles are commonly seen on flowers of the daisy family (Compositae) and umbellifers or at rest on the stumps or trunks of trees in the sun.

**Biology** The adults are herbivorous and feed at flowers. The common name for the family reflects their distinctive tumbling behaviour when disturbed. Larvae of *Tomoxia* species live in decaying wood while those of *Mordellistena* burrow in plant stems and may induce galls. The larvae of some species are predacious while others bore in the fruit bodies of fungi.

**Economic importance** Mordellids are not pests.

*Tomoxia biguttata*

BL

# Oil or Blister Beetles

**Order**  Coleoptera
**Family**  Meloidae
**Body length**  5–35mm (¼–1⅜in), mostly 10–18mm (⅜–¾in)
**Distribution**  Worldwide except New Zealand
**Number of species**  World–2000; NA–315; UK–9

**Identification**  Most oil beetles are black or brown but some
are metallic green or have red, yellow or white markings. Many
meloids have a leathery texture. Some species are elongate
while others can be very oval. The head is large, broadly
triangular and bent downwards. The pronotum is often
squarish and narrower than the back of the head and the front
of the elytra. The elytra of ground-living species can be very
short, exposing a large part of the swollen abdomen. Other
species can be nearly parallel-sided with the elytra reaching the
end of the abdomen.
**Habitat**  These beetles occur on flowers and foliage.
**Biology**  Many adult species are herbivorous and when
present in large numbers can cause total defoliation of host
plants. Many species have an interesting life-cycle. Females lay
large numbers of eggs in soil and the newly hatched,
predacious larvae seek out the eggs of grasshoppers or bees. In
other species, the larvae attach themselves to the bodies of
bees visiting flowers. When the female bee lays her eggs the
beetle larva sneaks into the cell with the egg and gets sealed in.
It eats the bee's egg and food provisions left by the parent bee.
The name blister beetle comes from the fact that they can
produce fluids capable of raising skin blisters. Species of the
genus *Meloe* are ground-living with short, overlapped elytra.
**Economic importance**  Some adult species can be pests of
crops such as potatoes, tomatoes, clovers and some root crops.
The medicinally useful substance, cantharidin, is extracted
commercially from the bright, metallic green elytra of *Lytta
vesicatoria* (Spanish Fly) and used in the treatment of some
urogenital illnesses. It is inadvisable to test the supposed
aphrodisiac properties
of cantharidin.

*Meloe proscarabeus*

BL

# Longhorn Beetles

**Order** Coleoptera
**Family** Cerambycidae
**Body length** 3–130mm (⅛–5in), most under 45mm (1¾in)
**Distribution** Worldwide, primarily tropical
**Number of species** World–25,000; NA–960; UK–60

**Identification** Members of this large and diverse family of beetles are brown or cryptically coloured but many can be brightly marked or have aposematic black, yellow or orange coloration. The most distinctive feature is the antennae which are often held backwards and are two-thirds to four times as long as the body. The body is elongate, cylindrical and often hairy although some small species might look superficially ant-like. The eyes are notched or completely divided and the antennae are often inserted within the notch.

**Habitat** The majority of adults can be found at flowers in a variety of terrestrial habitats. Nocturnal species can be found during the day under debris or bark.

**Biology** Adults feed on pollen and nectar at flowers, or on leaves, roots or wood but many species do not eat a great deal. Their eggs are laid in cracks and crevices in dead or living timber or the stems, twigs, branches or roots of woody plants and trees. The larvae burrow into the wood, feeding as they go. Their burrows are often large and always of circular cross-section. The larvae are elongate and cylindrical with very strong jaws and no, or very small, legs and may spend several years developing. Adults have been known to emerge from furniture. *Leptura*, *Strangalia* and *Grammoptera* are some of the many genera found across the northern hemisphere.

**Economic importance** Many species are serious pests of coniferous and deciduous trees. The genus *Saperda* contains several species injurious to apple, poplar and elm trees. *Hylotrupes bajulus* is the House Longhorn Beetle whose larvae can damage softwood timbers in buildings.

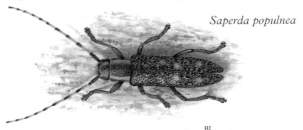

*Saperda populnea*

BL

# Pea and Bean Weevils

**Order** Coleoptera
**Family** Bruchidae
**Body length** 1–20mm (⅛–¾in), mostly under 10mm (⅜in)
**Distribution** Worldwide
**Number of species** World–1300; NA–135; UK–7

**Identification** These dull brown or black beetles are often mottled with patches of white or pale brown hairs or scales. They are oval or egg-shaped with a small head and slightly shortened elytra which expose the end of the abdomen. The head is often not visible from above and the jaws are carried on a short snout. The antennae are short and can appear comb-like or club-ended. The hind legs are often thickened and bear strong tooth-like projections.
**Habitat** Adults can be found on foliage, near leguminous plants or in stored pulses.
**Biology** Bruchids are not weevils, this common name is more correctly applied to the Curculionidae (p.107). The adults of all species lay their eggs on seeds. The larvae, which are whitish grubs with small heads and strong jaws, burrow inside where they spend their entire larval development. They pupate near the surface and chew their way out of the seed coat, leaving round holes. There can be many larvae developing inside one seed.
**Economic importance**
Many species are serious pests of stored peas, beans and leguminous field crops. *Acanthoscelides obtectus*, the Bean Weevil, *Bruchus pisorum*, the Pea Weevil and *Callosobruchus maculatus*, the Cowpea Weevil are all notorious and widespread species that can cause great economic losses.

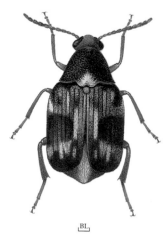

BL

*Callosobruchus maculatus*

# Leaf Beetles

*Leptinotarsa decemlineata*

BL

**Order** Coleoptera
**Family** Chrysomelidae
**Body length** 1–35mm (⅛–1⅜in), mostly 3–15mm (¼–⅝in)
**Distribution** Worldwide
**Number of species** World–30,000; NA–1480; UK–254

**Identification** The family is very large and there is a huge diversity of form, size and colour. The species of some genera are cylindrical and elongate while others look very like ladybirds. They can be distinguished by the fact that ladybirds have three clearly visible tarsal segments while leaf beetles have four. Typical leaf beetles are smooth, dorsally convex and many are brightly coloured or have a metallic lustre. Some species, called tortoise beetles (subfamily: Cassidinae), have lateral expansions of the body and the small, jumping flea beetles (subfamily: Alticinae) have very swollen hind legs.

**Habitat** Chrysomelids can be found on every plant species and in all terrestrial habitats. Species of the subfamily Donaciinae have aquatic larvae which feed on submerged plants and obtain their air from the stems.

**Biology** Adults and larvae of all species are herbivorous. The adults mainly graze or chew flowers and foliage while the grub-like, short-legged larvae can feed externally or mine and bore through leaves, stems and roots. Some species can overcome chemical plant defences by isolating parts of leaves before feeding. There are many important subfamilies, numerous genera and many species common across the northern hemisphere.

**Economic importance** Very many species are serious pests of all manner of plants and crops. The notorious Colorado Potato Beetle, *Leptinotarsa decemlineata*, which eats potatoes, tomatoes and aubergines and spreads plant diseases, is a member of this family and a serious pest on both sides of the Atlantic. The list of crops damaged by these beetles is very long but some species have been successfully used in the biological control of weeds.

# Snout Beetles or Weevils

**Order** Coleoptera
**Family** Curculionidae
**Body length** 1–48mm (⅛–1¾in), mostly under 20mm (¾in)
**Distribution** Worldwide
**Number of species** World–41,000; NA–2700; UK–400

**Identification** Weevils exhibit a huge diversity of size, shape and colour. Many are dull or cryptically coloured but others can have very brightly coloured bodies with metallic blue or green scales. All weevils have a snout called the rostrum, which is a prolongation of the head. The rostrum, which carries the jaws at its end, may be short and broad or long and thin. In some species, the rostrum is up to three times as long as the body. The antennae arise from either side of the snout and are nearly always elbowed with clubbed ends The elytra are very tough, often have a sculptured surface and in some species they are fused.

**Habitat** Curculionids are associated with virtually every species of plant on earth and occur in all terrestrial habitats. The larvae of a few species can be found inside the tissues of aquatic plants.

**Biology** Nearly all species are herbivorous and can be found eating every plant part from the roots up to the seeds. The female lays her eggs inside plant tissues and the pale, legless, grub-like larvae mainly feed internally or underground on roots, although a few species feed externally on foliage. *Apion*, *Otiorhynchus*, *Curculio*, *Anthonomus* and *Ceutorhynchus* are just a few of the genera common across the northern hemisphere.

**Economic importance** In a group of herbivorous insects of this size, it is no surprise that there are very many pest species. Many of the pest species are cosmopolitan. The Rice Weevil, *Sitophilus oryzae*, and the Grain Weevil, *S. granarius*, are pests of grain and grain products. The Cotton Boll Weevil, *Anthonomus grandis*, is the major pest species attacking the American cotton crop. The weevil prevents flower development by its feeding and can cause enormous losses.

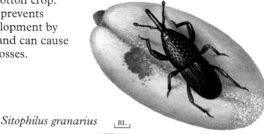

*Sitophilus granarius*   BL

# Bark Beetles

**Order** Coleoptera
**Family** Scolytidae
**Body length** 1–8mm (⅛–⅜in), mostly under 5mm (¼in)
**Distribution** Worldwide
**Number of species** World–9000; NA–500; UK–54

**Identification** Scolytids are fairly small, compact, brown or
black, cylindrical beetles. The head is sometimes visible from
above but in most cases it is concealed by the hood-like
pronotum. The body often has grooves or striations running
longitudinally and sculpturing in the form of small pits or
punctures. The antennae are short, elbowed and have very
distinct clubbed ends. The rear part of the elytra are concave,
or specially shaped to serve as a shovel.
**Habitat** These beetles are found in close association with a
large number of coniferous and deciduous tree species.
**Biology** Adults mate under the bark of trees and females
excavate one or more brood galleries in which they lay eggs.
The hatched larvae, which are fleshy and without legs, move
outwards from the brood gallery, eating as they go and making
a characteristic and often species-specific pattern under the
bark. Some species occur deeper inside the wood. Bark beetles
carry spores of particular fungi on their head and thorax.
When their eggs are laid the tree is infected and the fungus
spreads through the vessels of the wood, causing a brown or
blue stain. The fungal growth clogs up the vessels of the
sapwood and can kill the tree. The larvae feed on starches and
sugars in the wood and on the fungus introduced by their
parents. Many species produce chemical attraction odours
which lead to rapid and massive infestations. Ambrosia beetles
(*Xyleborus* spp.) tunnel in wood but the larvae simply feed on
the introduced fungus.
**Economic importance** Many
species are very serious pests of
commercial tree species. Bark
beetles were the vectors of the
dutch elm disease fungus that
removed elm trees from many
parts of Britain and North
America. Species of the genera
*Ips*, *Scolytus* and *Dendroctonus*
are notable.

*Polygraphus poligraphus*

BL

# Stylopids

**Order** Strepsiptera
**Family** Stylopidae
**Body length** 0.5–4mm (up to ¼in)
**Distribution** Worldwide
**Number of species** World–260; NA–80; UK–13

**Identification** These small insects are very strange-looking parasites of other insects. The males are dark-coloured, winged and look a bit like tiny beetles. They have protruding eyes and the antennae have between four and seven segments. The front wings are very reduced while the hind wings are large and fan-like with a few radiating veins. Females are grub-like with no wings or legs and never leave their hosts.
**Habitat** The males are free-living but the females are always found on their hosts.
**Biology** Most species of stylopid parasitize bees of the families Adrenidae and Halictidae while others use sphecid or vespid wasps as hosts. The males find unmated females by means of a sexual odour which they produce. The female stylopid partly protrudes from the body of her host and many hundreds of eggs may mature within her swollen body. After giving birth, the female dies. Normally, first-stage, active, six-legged larvae called triungulins are produced and leave the body of the female through a special brood passage. The triungulins crawl onto flowers where they wait for a passing host of the correct kind. They cling to the hairs of the host bee or wasp and, once inside the body, they moult to a legless form and begin to feed. The triungulins of some species may be ingested with a nectar meal. After several moults pupation occurs. Males emerge and fly away, females remain, usually sticking out between the abdominal segments.
**Economic importance** Although of considerable interest, stylopids are of no economic importance.

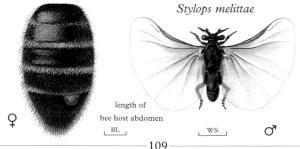

*Stylops melittae*

length of
bee host abdomen
⌐ BL ⌐

⌐ WS ⌐

♀        ♂

# Snow Scorpionflies

**Order** Mecoptera
**Family** Boreidae
**Body length** 2–8mm (⅛–⅜in), mostly 3–5mm (⅛–¼in)
**Distribution** Northern hemisphere
**Number of species** World–30; NA–13; UK–1

**Identification** These small insects are very dark brown or black in colour and are easily (but rarely) seen as they contrast strongly against a snowy background. The head, as in all Mecoptera, is prolonged downwards forming an obvious beak bearing the jaws. The antennae are quite long. The wings are very much reduced, resembling small hooks in the males or scales in females. The last abdominal segment of the female is much elongated for egg-laying.
**Habitat** Snow scorpionflies can be seen in autumn and winter on the surface of snow, among mosses or under stones, particularly in cold or mountainous regions.
**Biology** These insects are not commonly encountered but when present are noticeable on account of their colour and rapid walking and jumping. Males use their hook-like wings to hold and carry the females during mating. The eggs are laid in moss and the larvae look like small, curved caterpillars. They have well-developed thoracic legs and feed on moss and other plant matter. Superbly adapted for life in cold conditions, snow scorpionflies will die if held in the hand for too long. *Boreus* is the only widespread genus.
**Economic importance** These insects are of no economic importance.

*Boreus hyemalis*

BL

# Common Scorpionflies

**Order** Mecoptera
**Family** Panorpidae
**Body length** 9–25mm (³⁄₈–1in), mostly 15mm (⁵⁄₈in)
**Distribution** Worldwide but mainly holarctic
**Number of species** World–360; NA–40; UK–3

**Identification** The head of these brownish insects is produced downwards into a beak which carries strong-biting mouthparts. The wings are often marked with dark spots and bands and the hind wings are slightly smaller than the front wings. A very recognizable feature is the strange, upturned and bulbous genitalia of the males, from which the common name scorpionfly is derived. The abdomen of the females simply tapers towards the rear end and carries a pair of short cerci.
**Habitat** Common scorpionflies are found mainly on low-growing vegetation in shady places such as woodland margins.
**Biology** Adults feed mainly on dead or dying insects but sometimes also on nectar and fruit. Some species may rob spider webs of freshly caught prey and males may offer females items of food as nuptial gifts while copulation takes place. The eggs are laid in small groups in the soil and the larvae strongly resemble caterpillars. Larvae have three pairs of well-developed thoracic legs, eight pairs of very short abdominal 'feet' and may have spines or strong hairs. Pupation occurs underground in a cavity. All the species occurring in North America and Britain belong to the genus *Panorpa*. *Panorpa communis* and *P. germanica* are common in Europe, while *P. nebulosa* and *P. rufescens* are common in North America.
**Economic importance** Common scorpionflies are of no economic importance.

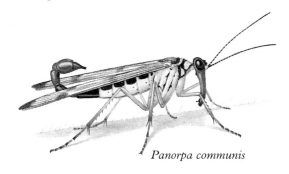

*Panorpa communis*

WS

# Common Fleas

**Order** Siphonaptera
**Family** Pulicidae
**Body length**
1–8mm (up to ⅜in)
**Distribution** Worldwide
**Number of species**
World–200; NA–16; UK–9

**Identification** All fleas are
easily recognized by their small
size, dark brown or black
coloration, winglessness and the great degree of lateral body
flattening. Fleas are very active jumpers and have enlarged
hind legs. The head is fused to a small thorax and has simple
eyes and short antennae in grooves at the side. The
mouthparts, which are short and strong, are modifed for
piercing the skin of their hosts and sucking blood. The body of
fleas is very hard and has rows of stout spines in various
places, the positions of which are diagnostic.

**Habitat** These fleas are found on the bodies of their
mammalian hosts although some species are confined to birds.

**Biology** This family includes species parasitic on dogs, cats,
man, hedgehogs, porcupines and rabbits as well as many other
carnivores and rodents. In general, fleas avoid light and are
attracted to the warmth and carbon dioxide given off by their
hosts. Small white eggs are deposited by the female in the nest
or sleeping places of their hosts. The larvae, which are minute,
slightly hairy and elongate, feed on the detritus in the host's
nest and will eat the faeces of the adult fleas and small
particles of dried blood. When fully grown the larva spins a
silken cocoon with tiny pieces of debris woven into the
structure. Many species are not very host-specific and will
attack a range of related animals. Many are cosmopolitan in
distribution. Some of the best-known species are the Cat Flea,
*Ctenocephalides felis*, the Dog Flea, *C. canis*, the Human Flea,
*Pulex irritans* and the Rat Flea, *Xenopsylla cheopis*. Many fleas
can jump considerable distances, the cat flea achieving a high
jump of 34cm (13in). The Human Flea has a generation time
of between four and six weeks.

**Economic importance** The black death or plague was
caused by the bacterium *Yersinia pestis* carried by the rat flea.
Many species can cause severe allergic reactions and transmit a
variety of diseases. The Dog Flea is the intermediate host for a
tapeworm which affect dogs, cats and man.

*BL* *Ctenocephalides felis*

# Crane Flies

**Order** Diptera
**Family** Tipulidae
**Body length** 6–60mm (¼–2⅜in),
mostly 12–24mm (½–1in)
**Distribution** Worldwide
**Number of species**
World–15,000; NA–1525; UK–318

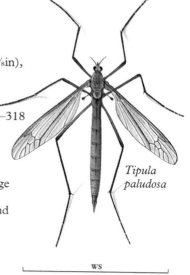

*Tipula
paludosa*

ws

**Identification** Crane flies
constitute the largest fly
family. Most are brown, black
or grey often with yellow, orange
or pale brown markings. The
body is elongate and slender and
there is a distinctive V-shaped
groove on top of the thorax.
The wings are long and often
have dark markings or spots.
Large species rest with wings
outstretched while smaller
species fold their wings back along the body. The antennae are
relatively long and in some species the male antennae have a
feathery appearance. A characteristic feature of these flies is
that their legs, which are very long and thin, are shed very
easily. A common name used for these flies is 'daddy long
legs'. The end of the abdomen is blunt in males whereas
females have a sharply pointed, tough ovipositor.

**Habitat** Adults are commonly found near water or among
rank vegetation. Many woodland species are common and very
abundant.

**Biology** Eggs are laid in the soil or in debris and the elongate,
cylindrical larvae, which are mostly brown or grey in colour,
may be aquatic, partially aquatic or terrestrial in habits. Adult
crane flies live for a few days and may not feed at all but some
species take nectar or similar fluid food through their slender
mouthparts. The larvae, called leatherjackets on account of the
texture of their bodies, are mainly herbivorous or
saprophagous but some aquatic species may be carnivorous.
Larval food includes all manner of decaying plant material,
debris, fungi, mosses and rotting wood. *Tipula*, *Limonia* and
*Nephrotoma* are among the many common genera.

**Economic importance** Many species are pests of grasses,
alfalfa, leguminous crops, garden plants and lawns.

# Moth Flies and Sand Flies

**Order** Diptera
**Family** Psychodidae
**Body length** 1.5–5mm (up to ¼in)
**Distribution** Nearly worldwide
**Number of species** World–1000; NA–91: UK–76

**Identification** These flies are small, moth-like and have their bodies, wings and legs covered with long hairs or scales. The wings, which are usually broad and with pointed tips, are held tent-like over the body or partly spread in moth flies (subfamily: Psychodinae) or together above the body in sand flies (subfamily: Phlebotominae). The flight of these flies is erratic and weak.

**Habitat** Damp or shaded places are common habitats for these flies and many species stay close to the larval breeding areas. Many species are attracted to lights after dark.

**Biology** Most species are nocturnal and rest during the day. The sand flies are sometimes regarded as a family distinct from the moth flies or owl midges, as they are sometimes known. Sand flies are blood-feeders, attacking some reptiles and a wide range of vertebrate animals including man. Their larvae are saprophagous soil-dwellers. The larvae of moth flies are found in decaying organic matter and can be found in drains and sewers in large numbers. Adult moth flies do not bite. The larval forms of many species are unknown and it is certain that many species are undescribed. Species of the sand fly genus *Lutzomyia* occur in North America but there are no sand flies in Britain. Of the moth flies, species of *Psychoda* and *Pericoma* are common across the northern hemisphere.

**Economic importance** In many tropical and subtropical regions of the world, sand flies, particularly species of the genus *Phlebotomus*, are very serious vectors of leishmaniasis.

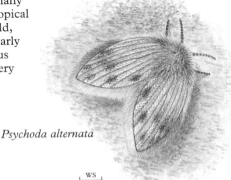

*Psychoda alternata*

WS

# Mosquitoes

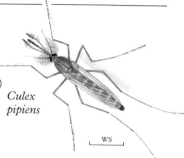

**Order** Diptera
**Family** Culicidae
**Body length** 3–9mm (⅛–⅜in)
**Distribution** Worldwide,
mainly warmer regions
**Number of species**
World–3100; NA–150; UK–36

*Culex
pipiens*

WS

**Identification** These very slender, delicate flies have small
heads with elongate, slender, sucking mouthparts. The body is
covered with tiny scales and appears pale brown to reddish-
brown. The wings, which may be clear or with fine, dark
markings, are long and narrow with scales along the veins and
margins. The antennae are feathery in males and slightly hairy
in females. As they fly their high-pitched whine gives away
their presence. Two important subfamilies can be recognized
by the way they rest. Anopheline mosquitoes rest with their
heads down, their mouthparts straight out and the body
inclined at 45° to the surface, whereas the Culicinae rest
horizontal to the surface and the mouthparts bent down.
**Habitat** Larval mosquitoes occur in virtually every aquatic
habitat. Adults are common at dusk in woodland and forest.
**Biology** Females are blood-suckers, feeding on a wide range
of vertebrate hosts. Males do not bite but occasionally feed on
nectar or honeydew. Eggs are laid singly or in floating groups
of 40–300 eggs, called rafts, on the surface of any body of
water. Any water will do, from rain-filled containers and tree
holes to ponds and lakes. The larvae, which are called
wrigglers from the way they thrash about in the water, are
mostly saprophagous, although some are predacious. In most
species, air is obtained from the surface but some larvae get
their oxygen from aquatic plants. The life-cycle takes between
15 and 20 days. *Anopheles*, *Aedes* and *Culex* are important and
widely distributed genera.
**Economic importance** Many mosquitoes are very serious
disease vectors in many parts of the world. Among human
diseases they transmit are malaria, yellow fever, dengue,
filariasis and encephalitis. Around the world about two million
people die from malaria every year. Even when these flies do
not carry diseases, their bites can be painful and cause allergic
reactions and sores. Control measures include habitat drainage
and insecticides, but personal protection can be achieved by
the use of fly screens, suitable clothing and repellants.

# Non-biting Midges

**Order** Diptera
**Family** Chironomidae
**Body length** 1–9mm (up to ⅜in)
**Distribution** Worldwide
**Number of species** World–5000;
NA–820; UK–400

*Chironomus plumosus*

ws

**Identification** These pale green, brown or grey midges are delicate, gnat-like flies that look a little like mosquitoes but do not have scales on the wings and the mouthparts are very short or absent. The males have very feathery antennae and a slender body while females have hairy antennae and a stoutish body. The head is often concealed from above by the thorax. The legs and antennae are long and the wings are elongate and narrow.
**Habitat** Chironomids are common everywhere and can be seen in large swarms at dusk around ponds, lakes and streams.
**Biology** The short-lived adults do not bite and live for a week or two. The majority of the two- or three-year life-cycle is spent as a larva. Mating occurs in swarms and the eggs are laid in a mass of jelly-like substance on the surface of water or on vegetation. The larvae are elongate, cylindrical and usually green, brown or yellow in colour. They feed on decayed organic material and small plants or aquatic animals. The larvae can be free-living in detritus or live in specially made tubes in the bottom mud, although the larvae of a few species line the leaves of water plants. The larvae of some species are called blood worms and are red due to the presence of haemoglobin in their body fluids. These larvae live in stagnant ponds or water with a low oxygen content. There are many genera common across the northern hemisphere including *Diamesa*, *Cricotopus*, *Chironomus* and *Polypedilum*.
**Economic importance** Besides being an important source of food for many aquatic animals, chironomids are used as indicators of water quality. Some species are very tolerant of pollution while others are not.

# Biting Midges

**Order** Diptera
**Family** Ceratopogonidae
**Body length** 1–6mm (up to ¼in), mostly around 3mm (⅛in)
**Distribution** Worldwide, mainly northern hemisphere
**Number of species** World–2000; NA–460; UK–165

**Identification** Similar in general appearance to the Chironomidae, these slender or robust flies are somewhat smaller and often have dark patterns on their wings. The head is not concealed from above by the thorax. The mouthparts are short and piercing. The wings are broader than in non-biting midges and are held together flat over the body at rest.
**Habitat** Common near the shore, at the margins of ponds, rivers, lakes and in boggy areas, adults do not fly more than 100m(328ft) from their breeding grounds.
**Biology** The adults of most species are active blood-suckers and because of their small size they are often called 'no-see-ums'. Species of the genus *Forcipomyia* suck the body fluids of much larger insects, while others catch and eat smaller insects. The eggs are laid in groups or long strings covered with a jelly-like substance and the slender, worm-like larvae can be aquatic, semi-aquatic in mud or soil, or terrestrial, under bark or in debris. Most species are active at dusk and both sexes of some species will take nectar for energy. Large swarms of these tiny flies have a characteristic dancing motion.
**Economic importance** The most notorious human-biters belong to the genus *Culicoides*. Anyone who has wondered why large areas of Scotland have remained so unspoilt need look only as far as the nearest bog to find the answer, *C. punctatum*, the dreaded Scottish midge. In some parts of the world, biting midges are vectors of filarial worms, protozoan blood parasites and viruses.

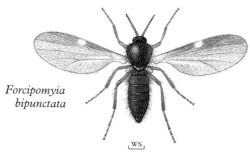

*Forcipomyia bipunctata*

WS

# Black Flies

**Order** Diptera
**Family** Simuliidae
**Body length** 1–5mm (⅛–¼in), mostly under 4mm (¼in)
**Distribution** Worldwide
**Number of species** World–1500; NA–150; UK–37

**Identification** Black flies are black or dark brown in general body colour but some can be reddish-brown, grey or yellowish-orange. The body of these flies is distinctively stout and the thorax has a humped appearance. The head is relatively large with short, robust mouthparts, which in females are designed for cutting skin and sucking blood. The antennae and legs are short. The wings are broad at their bases and become narrow towards the ends with strong veins at the leading wing margin.
**Habitat** The adults can be found around various fast-flowing bodies of water where their larvae develop.
**Biology** The females of certain species require a blood meal before they can lay eggs. Eggs are laid on plants or stones above or below water. The aquatic larvae are attached to stones, twigs and large pieces of debris by means of hooks or a sucker device at the end of their abdomens. They filter and eat tiny organic particles and organisms from the water with special bristles around the mouth. The larvae pupate in conical cases attached to submerged sticks or stones. *Simulium* and *Prosimulium* species can be found on both sides of the Atlantic.
**Economic importance** Many species are serious pests and are vectors of various diseases. *Simulium damnosum* is the vector for river blindness in Africa (onchocerciasis). In general their bites produce toxic and allergic reactions and transmit a variety of parasitic organisms to man, birds and many other animals. In temperate regions of the northern hemisphere they do not transmit disease to man.

*Simulium austeni*

WS

# March Flies

**Order** Diptera
**Family** Bibionidae
**Body length** 5–11mm (¼–⅜in)
**Distribution** Worldwide
**Number of species** World–780; NA–78; UK–19

**Identification** These flies are stout-bodied, black or dark brown insects often with very hairy bodies and shortish legs. The heads of males and females are very different in design. The heads of males are larger and have large compound eyes which meet on top of the head. Females have smaller heads and eyes which do not meet. The short antennae which arise low on the head are made up of 8–16 bead-like segments. The wings, which are large with strong veins at the front margin, often have a pale brown tinge.

**Habitat** March flies are common on flowers in pastures, gardens and similar habitats during spring and early summer.

**Biology** The common name is a corruption of St Mark's fly. St Mark's Day falls on April 25, about the time when large mating swarms of these flies can be seen. Mated females dig down through the soil and lay 200–300 eggs in a small chamber. The scavenging larvae, which are elongate, slightly flattened with a large head and strong mouthparts, eat all manner of organic material, including plant roots. Larvae can be found in rich soil, compost heaps, dung, leaf litter and meadows. Pupation takes place underground in an earthen cell. The genus *Bibio* is the biggest in the northern hemisphere.

**Economic importance** Species whose larvae are root-feeders can be pests of cereal and vegetable crops and, in addition, can damage pastures and plant seedlings.

*Bibio marci*

WS

# Gall Midges

**Order** Diptera
**Family** Cecidomyiidae
**Body length** 1–8mm (up to ⅜in), mostly under 4mm (¼in)
**Distribution** Worldwide
**Number of species** World–4600; NA–1060; UK–620

**Identification** These very small, fragile flies are slender with long legs. The antennae are multi-segmented and thread-like with conspicuous whorls of hairs on each segment. The wings can be hairy and the reduced venation, with only a few unbranched longitudinal veins, is characteristic of the family. The eyes of both sexes touch or nearly touch on top of the head and, in some species, the eyes are divided into portions.
**Habitat** Cecidomyiids can be found in virtually any terrestrial habitat around decaying organic matter, fungi or plants.
**Biology** Although a very large number of gall midges induce galls on plants, the larvae of some are free-living. The habits of larvae are very varied between species, some are predacious or parasitic on small insect mites, others are saprophagous, others live in fungi, flowers and other parts of plants and some live in galls made by other insects. Larvae are white, yellow or red and lack any clear features except a structure called the sternal spatula or 'breast plate'. Gall-forming species lay their eggs in particular parts of specific host plants and induce a characteristic simple gall inside which the larvae grow. Plants of the daisy, grass and willow families are most commonly galled in North America and Europe. Species of *Rhabdophaga*, *Dasineura* and *Contarinia* are numerous and widespread across the northern hemisphere.

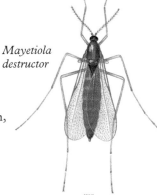

*Mayetiola destructor*

**Economic importance** Many species are pests. Larvae of the Hessian Fly, *Mayetiola destructor*, bore into the stems of wheat, rye and barley. The Pear Midge, *Contarinia pyrivora*, is a pest on both sides of the Atlantic. Sorghum, grapes, clovers and some conifers are damaged by these flies.

WS

# Fungus Gnats

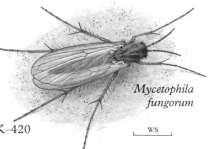

**Order** Diptera
**Family** Mycetophilidae
**Body length**
2–13mm (¹/₈–⁵/₈in)
**Distribution** Worldwide
**Number of species**
World–3000; NA–720; UK–420

*Mycetophila
fungorum*

WS

**Identification** Fungus gnats are mosquito-like flies with a black, brown or dull yellow coloration. Some species may be brightly coloured with conspicuous wing markings. The head appears flattened from front to back and the antennae are generally long although the females of some species may have very short antennae. Good recognition features are the humped thorax and the long legs, which arise from very elongate coxae. The thorax and tibiae have strong bristle-like hairs and the tibiae have apical spurs. The hind legs are modified for jumping.

**Habitat** Adult fungus gnats are commonly found in moist, wooded areas but are also found in houses.

**Biology** The adults of some species have elongate mouthparts and feed at flowers or on honeydew. The eggs are laid singly or in small groups on the food substrate. The slender, cylindrical larvae are soft and white with a dark head and mostly eat fungal matter. They are found living gregariously in fleshy or woody fungi, decaying organic matter, in dead wood, under bark or in the nests of birds and other animals. Some unusual cave-dwelling species emit light and lure small insects into silk traps. Pupation occurs inside the host fungus or in a loose cocoon made of soil particles and silk. The larvae of some species are predacious on tiny insects and worms. *Exechia*, *Mycetophila* and *Phronia* are common and widespread genera.

**Economic importance** The larvae of some species can be pests by damaging the roots of wheat seedlings, cucumbers and potted plants. Although most fungus gnats attack wild fungi, some species can cause immense damage to cultivated mushroom beds.

# Horse Flies

*Tabanus bovinus*

**Order** Diptera
**Family** Tabanidae
**Body length** 6–28mm (¼–1¼in)
**Distribution** Worldwide
**Number of species**
World–4100; NA–350; UK–28

**Identification** Horse flies, which are also called deer flies, clegs and gadflies, are very stout-bodied, hairless and fast-flying insects with distinctive large heads and eyes. They are black, grey or brown and have broad abdomens which often have bright yellow or orange bands or other markings. The large, flattened, hemispherical head is the most distinctive feature of the family. The antennae are short and the large eyes occupy most of the head. The eyes of males meet on top of the head while those of females are slightly separated. The eyes of both sexes are green or purple and have iridescent bands and spots. The blade-like mouthparts of females are adapted for cutting skin. The wings are often patterned with pale or dark markings.

**Habitat** Adults may fly a long way from the wet, larval breeding grounds and are commonly found around mammals.

**Biology** The eggs are laid on vegetation near water in small groups or in marshy areas. The larvae are predacious on small worms, crustaceans and insect larvae and may be aquatic or live in very damp soil, litter or rotting wood. They hibernate as fully grown larvae and pupate in spring to emerge and mate in early summer. Adult females feed on the blood of mammals and birds and approach their victim with great stealth, often feeding in hard-to-reach places. Their bites are very painful. Males are not blood-feeders and can be seen taking nectar at flowers. Many species of deer flies (*Chrysops*) and horse flies (*Tabanus* and *Hybomitra)* are widespread and common.

**Economic importance** In some parts of the world, tabanids are vectors of bacterial, viral, filarial and protozoal diseases in man and animals but these problems are insignificant in the northern hemisphere. They can be very troublesome to domestic and other animals and sensitive humans can suffer large swellings and allergic reactions.

# Soldier Flies

*Sargus cuprarius*

**Order** Diptera
**Family** Stratiomyidae
**Body length** 2–17mm (⅛–¾in)
**Distribution** Worldwide
**Number of species** World–1800;
NA–260; UK–50

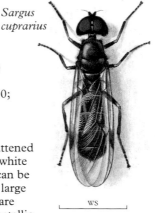

ws

**Identification** Stratiomyids are
normally quite robust, slightly flattened
flies with bright yellow, green or white
markings. Species of this family can be
variable in appearance; some are large
and look like wasps while others are
smaller and coloured brown or metallic
bluish-black. The broad abdomen often has patterns of
contrasting yellow, black or green bands or stripes. The thorax
can be very hairy. The head, which is as broad as the thorax, is
hemispherical or very rounded. The eyes occupy a large area
of the head, especially in males, and the stout antennae are
distinctive, with the third segment annulated and held bent
outwards from the basal segments. The majority of the wing
veins occur near the leading edge and the wings are folded flat
over the body at rest. They are not strong fliers but some can
hover like hover flies.
**Habitat** Adults prefer damp areas and can be seen sitting on
flowers of willow, hawthorn, daisies and umbellifers.
**Biology** Soldier fly eggs are laid on plants near water, on the
surface of water or in dung, moss, leaf litter, soil and decaying
wood. The larvae are elongate and flattened, with tough,
leathery bodies impregnated with calcareous deposits.
Terrestrial larvae are saprophagous or carnivorous, attacking
bark beetles and the larvae of other flies. Aquatic larvae
breathe through spiracles at their rear end, the spiracles being
surrounded by a circle of hairs which close the opening when
submerged. Some aquatic larvae can tolerate high salinity and
even hot springs. Species of *Sargus*, *Stratiomys* and *Oxycera* are
typical of the northern hemisphere.
**Economic importance** Some soil-living larvae may damage
the roots of potatoes, lettuce and grasses. Larvae living under
bark may control bark beetle numbers.

# Robber or Assassin Flies

**Order** Diptera
**Family** Asilidae
**Body length** 3–50mm (⅛–2in), mostly 8–14mm (⅜–⅝in)
**Distribution** Worldwide
**Number of species** World–5000; NA–900; UK–27

**Identification** Robber flies are brownish or black with yellow or reddish-orange markings. The body may be slender, elongate, tapering and relatively hairless or stout, bee-like and very hairy or bristly. The head appears slightly hollowed between the widely separated, bulging eyes and the face has a conspicuous tuft of long hairs called the beard. The forward-pointing proboscis is stout and sharp for stabbing and sucking. The antennae are short and held erect. The legs are very strong, bristly and are designed for grasping other insects in flight. The wings are clear or with smoky tinges or patches.
**Habitat** Asilids can be found in a variety of terrestrial habitats and tend to be locally distributed.
**Biology** The larval biology of many species is unknown but in general they are cryptically coloured, elongate and taper at both ends. They are predators or scavengers in soil, leaf litter, rotting wood and other microhabitats close to the ground. The eggs, larvae and pupae of other insects are the usual diet of robber fly larvae. Adults are active in the sunshine in open or wooded areas and catch all manner of insects on the wing. Prey items which can often be very large, such as bees, dragonflies and grasshoppers are quickly stabbed and protein-dissolving and neurotoxic saliva is injected. The body contents of the paralysed insect are sucked up. Tough bodies and other insect defences are no match for these rapacious hunters.
*Lasiopogon*, *Stenopogon*, *Asilus* and *Leptogaster* are genera typical of the northern hemisphere.
**Economic importance** Careless handling of live asilids can result in a very painful bite. The service these insects might give in eating harmful species is balanced by their consumption of beneficial ones.

*Dioctria baumhaueri*  └ ws ┘

# Bee Flies

**Order** Diptera
**Family** Bombyliidae
**Body length** 2–28mm (⅛–1⅛in), mostly under 18mm (¾in)
**Distribution** Worldwide
**Number of species** World–5000; NA–800; UK–12

**Identification** Bee flies are stout-bodied and very hairy, resembling, as their name implies, bees. Body colour is usually brown, red and yellow and some can be brightly marked. The head is transverse or rounded and the mouthparts, which are often very long, are adapted for sucking nectar from long-tubed flowers. The thorax may be flat or slightly humped and the abdomen can be very broad and rounded or slightly elongated. The legs are slender and quite long and the wings may be clear or have dark bands or markings, particularly at the leading edge.
**Habitat** Bombyliids can be found feeding and flying around flowers in open, sunny areas or resting on sandy ground.
**Biology** In flight, bee flies sound and look like bees. Adults of both sexes are nectar-feeders but their larvae are parasitic on the larvae of solitary bees and wasps, beetles, moths and other fly species. The larvae of some species eat the eggs·of grasshoppers in the soil. Very little is known of the life history of many species. Female bombyliids produce a large number of small eggs. In *Bombylius* species, eggs are laid near the host bee nest and the young larvae enter to parasitize the bee larvae. The bee fly pupates inside the bee's cell and breaks its way out as an adult.
**Economic importance** Some are beneficial in the natural control of pest insects but some also kill beneficial species.

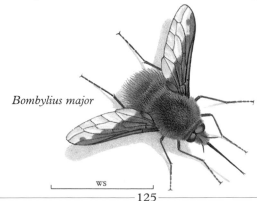

*Bombylius major*

ws

# Dance Flies

**Order** Diptera
**Family** Empidae
**Body length** 1.5–11mm ($\frac{1}{8}$–$\frac{3}{8}$in)
**Distribution** Worldwide, mainly northern hemisphere
**Number of species**
World–3500; NA–730; UK–350

*Dolichocephala irrorata*

**Identification** Species in this family are variable in appearance. Most of them are small and hairy with a stout thorax and a tapering, elongate abdomen. The general colour varies from dark brown and black to yellow or light brown. The head does not have a facial beard, is rounded or almost spherical and bears large eyes and a stiff, downward-pointing proboscis. The legs, which are long and slender, are used for grasping prey and, in males, the front tibiae and tarsi may be thickened or enlarged.

**Habitat** Dance flies can be found on vegetation in moist habitats, resting on tree trunks or on or near water.

**Biology** All dance fly adults are predacious, mainly catching and eating small flies. The common name comes from the mating swarms that periodically occur in which males fly up and down in a dancing fashion. Males may offer prey items to females to eat while mating takes place. The nuptial gifts are wrapped in silk or froth produced by special glands in the front tarsi of the males. Some females will not catch prey themselves but live entirely on nuptial gifts presented by the males during repeated matings. Some dance flies will take prey from spider webs or from the surface of water. Dance fly larvae are probably all predacious and live in humus, leaf litter, decaying wood and vegetation, under bark or in water. They are spindle-shaped with a retractible head and consume such items as black fly larvae in moss, coccids and mites. There are many species of *Platypalpus*, *Rhamphomyia*, *Hilara* and *Empis* across the northern hemisphere.

**Economic importance** Many species are probably very beneficial in controlling natural populations of pest insects such as mosquitoes.

# Long-legged Flies

**Order** Diptera
**Family** Dolichopodidae
**Body length** 0.8–7mm (up to ⅜in), most under 4mm (¼in)
**Distribution** Worldwide
**Number of species** World–5500; NA–1230; UK–270

**Identification** Dolichopodids are small or very small flies with a metallic or very shiny green, yellow or blue-green colour and bristly bodies. The head is rounded, globular or somewhat flattened and has a short, fleshy proboscis. The abdomen may be elongate and slightly flattened or shorter and more cylindrical. In males, the genitalia are large and held curved forward under the abdomen, while in females the abdomen ends in a sharp point. There is a considerable degree of sexual dimorphism in these flies. Males have all manner of hairy tufts and other ornamentation on the tarsi, antennae and other parts of the body which are used as sexual signals to the females during mating.

**Habitat** Long-legged flies are common in moist habitats, meadows, woodland, stream and lake margins and species of several genera are found at the seashore.

**Biology** Adults are mostly predacious on small soft-bodied insects which they squeeze and chew with their fleshy mouthparts before sucking the juices. Many species can be seen at flowers feeding on nectar. Larval biology is not well known but they are mainly predacious and live in wet soil, under bark, leaf litter, seaweed or in water. The larvae are white, cylindrical and taper towards the front end where there is a retractible head. The body has tiny pseudopods with spines which help the larvae to move through their substrate. Larvae of *Medetera* species are predacious on bark beetle larvae. Despite elaborate courtship rituals, the males of many species will attempt to mate with females of the wrong species or members of different genera.

**Economic importance**
Adults of the genus *Dolichopus* are useful as predators of mosquito larvae. Many others are of importance in controlling natural populations of soft-bodied insect pests.

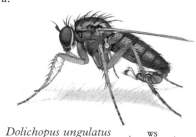

*Dolichopus ungulatus*      ∟ ws ⌐

127

# Humpbacked or Scuttle Flies

**Order** Diptera
**Family** Phoridae
**Body length** 0.6–6mm (up to ¼in)
**Distribution** Worldwide
**Number of species** World–2800; NA–360; UK–277

**Identification** These small dark brown, black or yellowish flies have a distinctive humpbacked appearance because the head is so strongly turned downwards. The head is small, sometimes rather short or flattened, and carries antennae which have the appearance of having only one segment. The other segments are small and concealed. The wings are fairly large, clear or light brown and only have strongly marked veins towards the front edge. In females of some species the wings are often absent or very reduced, forming narrow straps. The hind femora are often very stout, enlarged and flattened. The bristles of the body, if looked at under a powerful lens, have a feathery appearance.

**Habitat** Adult scuttle flies are common around decaying animal or plant matter such as compost heaps, carcasses and rotting fungi. Other places where phorids might be seen include flowers, the burrows or nests of rodents, ants, bees, termites and wasps or around dung.

**Biology** The common name, scuttle fly, is derived from the fast, jerky running movements of the adults. The eggs are laid in decaying matter of all kinds including dead animals. The larvae of some species are associated with the nests of ants and termites while others can be internal parasites of insects, spiders, snails or millipedes. The very large genus *Megaselia* is cosmopolitan.

**Economic importance**
Generally, these insects are of no significant economic importance but there have been reports of wounds becoming infected and cases where the digestive tract of humans has been invaded. Phorids can sometimes be a minor pest in cultivated mushroom beds.

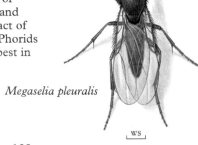

*Megaselia pleuralis*

# Hover or Flower Flies

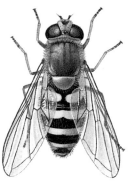

**Order** Diptera
**Family** Syrphidae
**Body length** 3–34mm (⅛–1⅜in),
mostly 10–20mm (⅜–¾in)
**Distribution** Worldwide
**Number of species** World–6000;
NA–870; UK–245

**Identification** Hover flies are
among the most easily recognized
and common species of all the
Diptera. The adults can be blue,
black or metallic and many have

*Syrphus vitripennis*
ws

strong yellow stripes, spots or bands. Some species are
relatively hairy and mimic bees, while others are smooth and
resemble wasps. The wings have a characteristic false vein
running down the middle of the wing (a simple thickening of
the membrane) and a false margin at the edge of the wing (the
interconnection of the outer wing veins). These flies are most
easily spotted in the field by their superb flying skills as they
hover and dart between flowers.
**Habitat** Hover flies are found at flowers in a wide range of
terrestrial habitats.
**Biology** Adult hover flies feed on pollen and nectar while
their larvae may be carnivorous, herbivorous or saprophagous.
The slug-like larvae of many species, such as those of *Syrphus,*
are voracious consumers of aphids and may eat thousands
during their development. Other species eat coccids, sawfly
larvae and many other soft-bodied pest species. Saprophagous
species live in rotting wood, dung, mud or dirty water. Aquatic
species such as those of *Eristalis* have an extensible posterior
siphon through which they breathe surface air. The larvae of
*Volucella* species live in the nests of bees and social wasps,
where they eat diseased larvae and pupae. Despite their bee or
wasp-like looks and behaviour, hover flies do not sting.
**Economic importance** The larvae of some species are
herbivorous and can damage the bulbs of ornamental and
garden flowers. In North America, the larvae of *Mesogramma
polita* can sometimes do damage to corn crops. Apart from
these minor problems, the vast majority of hover fly species are
of immense value in controlling pests and as pollinators.

# Fruit Flies

*Ceratitis capitata*

**Order** Diptera
**Family** Tephritidae
**Body length**
2–20mm (⅛–¾in), mostly
under 15mm (⅝in)
**Distribution** Worldwide
**Number of species**
World–4500; NA–280; UK–72

**Identification** Fruit flies are easily
recognizable by the very attractive
marbled and often intricate patterns
of dark wing markings. The picture
wing patterning, as it is often called, can be in the form of
transverse bands, interrupted patches or zigzag stripes. The
female abdomen tapers and ends in a pointed, rigid ovipositor,
while in males the abdomen is blunt or round-ended and does
not taper. In females of *Toxotrypana* the ovipositor can be
longer than the rest of the body.
**Habitat** These flies are common around all manner of
flowers and vegetation.
**Biology** During courtship, the males of many species walk
about in front of the females displaying their patterned wings
by waving one slowly and holding the other upright. The
larvae of all tephritids are herbivorous, living inside soft fruits,
in the flower heads of daisies and related plants, as stem- or
leaf-miners in umbelliferous and other plants or as gall-
formers. The eggs are invariably laid inside the plant tissue
and, when fully grown, the larvae have a very rounded
appearance. There are many genera common to the northern
hemisphere such as *Tephritis*, *Urophora* and *Trypeta*.
**Economic importance** There are several important pest
species, of which the best known is the Mediterranean Fruit
Fly, *Ceratitis capitata*. This species is a very serious tropical
pest of citrus and other soft fruits such as peaches and
cherries. The larvae of *Rhagoletis* spp. bore inside apples and
other commercial and wild-growing fruit. Other important
crop plants attacked by these small flies include melon, celery,
aubergine, walnut and sunflower. Some species are beneficial
in biological control programmes against certain weeds.

# Rust Flies

**Order** Diptera
**Family** Psilidae
**Body length** 3–8mm (⅛–⅜in)
**Distribution** Primarily northern hemisphere
**Number of species** World–250; NA–35; UK–28

**Identification** Rust flies are slender or moderately robust and reddish-brown to black in colour. The head is slightly triangular or rounded and the antennae may be relatively long. The basal area of the wings has a small pale ridge or streak running horizontally, but this is difficult to see. The body does not have strong bristles, and in some species is virtually bare.
**Habitat** Adult rust flies can be found near their host plants and prefer shady, damp, well-vegetated areas.
**Biology** The eggs are laid on or in the host plants and the larvae may be found boring through stems or roots and under the bark of trees. The larvae and their habits are not well known but they are generally smooth, slender and herbivorous. Some species induce galls on their host plants. The common name is derived from the fact that parts of affected plants may turn rust-coloured and peel off in flakes. *Loxocera*, *Psila* and *Chyliza* are genera common to both sides of the Atlantic.
**Economic importance** The well-known Carrot Root Fly, *Psila rosae*, whose larvae damage the roots of carrot, celery and other umbelliferous plants, can be a serious pest. The adult is 4mm (¼in) long and shiny black with a reddish-yellow head and yellow legs.

*Psila rosae*

WS

# Black Scavenger or Ensign Flies

**Order** Diptera
**Family** Sepsidae
**Body length** 2–6mm (⅛–¼in)
**Distribution** Worldwide
**Number of species** World–250; NA–35; UK–26

**Identification** Members of this small family are slender flies
with a shiny black, purple or reddish body colour, narrow
wings and longish, slender legs. The wings of most species are
clear and have a readily identifiable, small dark spot at the
ends. The head is rounded or globular and the eyes are quite
large. The front legs of males have special bristles, spines or
other structures which are used to grip the wings of the
females during mating. The abdomen is constricted where it
joins the thorax and looks vaguely wasp-like. Some small
species look superficially like ants.
**Habitat** These flies are common on flowers, vegetation,
around dung or decaying plant or animal matter.
**Biology** Adult sepsids are flower-feeders but the larvae are
saprophagous and have been found in dung and rotting
organic matter. Adult males gather in quite large numbers on
vegetation and display their wing tips by walking back and
forth, flicking their wings outwards. This behaviour is a sexual
signal to the females and a prelude to mating. Although a
small family, some species may be locally very abundant and
several genera are widespread. *Nemopoda*, *Themira* and *Sepsis*
are typical genera of the northern hemisphere.
**Economic importance** No sepsid species are of significant
economic importance.

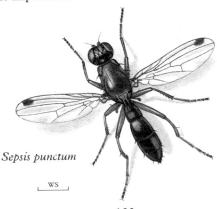

*Sepsis punctum*

WS

# Heleomyzids

**Order**  Diptera
**Family**  Heleomyzidae
**Body length**  2–10mm (⅛–⅜in), mostly 3–7mm (⅛–⅜in)
**Distribution**  Probably worldwide
**Number of species**  World–500; NA–115; UK–60

**Identification**  The majority of species are brown but others can be yellowish to reddish-brown or black. The body is moderately bristly and the wings are clear or with a faint brownish or yellowish tinge or faint spots.
**Habitat**  Heleomyzids are common flies around rank vegetation and prefer shady, moist habitats such as woodlands. Many species are found close to the larval breeding sites.
**Biology**  The elongate larvae of these flies are whitish or yellowish and taper markedly towards the front end. The biology of many species is not known but in general they are saprophagous and can be found in decaying plant or animal matter, dung, animal corpses, fungi and a large range of other situations. Some species have been found in the burrows of mammals, the nests of birds and bat caves. Most of the genera recorded in North America occur across the northern hemisphere. Species of *Heleomyza* and *Suilla* are typical.
**Economic importance**  The larvae of *Suilla lurida* are known to attack onion and garlic plants.

*Heleomyza serrata*

ws

# Small Dung Flies

**Order** Diptera
**Family** Sphaeroceridae
**Body length** 1–5mm (up to ¼in)
**Distribution** Worldwide
**Number of species** World–950; NA–120; UK–110

**Identification** These flies are small, stout-bodied and brown, black or yellowish in body colour. The head and legs are often yellow. The wings may be broad or narrow and, in some species, may be absent altogether. A good recognition feature, although difficult to see without a powerful lens, is the first segment of the hind tarsus which is much thicker than the other segments.
**Habitat** Sphaerocerids prefer moist conditions, commonly seen around manure, refuse piles and similar locations.
**Biology** The adults are often very abundant and lay their eggs in all manner of decaying organic matter. The larvae of most species are slender and taper towards the front end. The biology of many species is not known. Among the larval breeding sites that have been recorded are dung piles, nests of mammals, rotting seaweed, sewage works and compost heaps. Some species are known to cling to the bodies of dung beetles and thus gain access to their burrows to lay eggs. *Copromyza* and *Leptocera* are typical northern hemisphere genera.
**Economic importance** Although there have been reports of these flies acting as vectors for roundworm infections in mushroom beds and being minor pests in the food industry, they are of no great economic importance. As members of the dung community, they are certainly useful in the recycling of nutrients.

*Sphaerocera curvipes*

ws

# Leaf-mining Flies

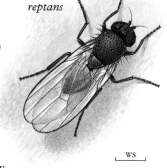

*Agromyza reptans*

**Order** Diptera
**Family** Agromyzidae
**Body length** 1–6mm (up to ¼in)
**Distribution** Worldwide, mainly northern hemisphere
**Number of species**
World–2500; NA–493; UK–300

**Identification** These small to medium-sized flies may be grey, black or sometimes greenish-yellow.

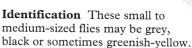

ws

The head and thorax are moderately hairy and the wings, which are relatively large, are usually clear. The abdomen is distinctly tapered and females have a rigid, pointed ovipositor. There are no clear and simple recognition features to aid the beginner but the works of the larvae are unmistakable.
**Habitat** Agromyzids are common flies on all types of vegetation and in a wide range of habitats.
**Biology** Adults lay their eggs in living plant tissue and in the best-known species the larvae make mines by chewing channels between the upper and lower surfaces of leaves. Some other species bore or mine in stems, seeds, roots or even the twigs of trees. Most species are monophagous, others are oligophagous and very few are polyphagous. In many cases, the shape of the larval mine, the frass that the larva produces and the host plant species are characteristic of a particular agromyzid species. The mines increase in width as the larva grows and may be linear, blotch-like, serpentine, circular or irregular. There may be several generations per year and pupation takes place on the ground. Species of *Agromyza*, *Liriomyza* and *Phytomyza* are common throughout the northern hemisphere. *Phytomyza ilicis* is the familiar Holly Leaf Miner.
**Economic importance** Many species are pests and well over 100 crops plants, such as beans, corn, alfalfa, cabbage, tomatoes, cucumber and celery, around the world are damaged by the larvae of these small flies. A few species have been used in the biological control of weed species.

# Shore Flies

**Order** Diptera
**Family** Ephydridae
**Body length** 2–11mm (⅛–⅜in), mostly under 9mm (⅜in)
**Distribution** Worldwide, mainly northern hemisphere
**Number of species** World–1400; NA–430; UK–130

**Identification** Many species are dark grey or black and can be shiny or dull. The wings are usually clear but can be patterned in some species. The face can appear somewhat bulging. The degree of hairiness and ornamentation in these flies is very variable indeed and makes it almost impossible to give clear recognition features.
**Habitat** Marshes, wet meadows, the seashore and the margins of ponds, lakes and rivers are typical habitats.
**Biology** The larvae are semi-aquatic or aquatic. Most species prefer fresh water but some can tolerate the high salt concentration of brackish water, salt marshes and the alkaline water of desert lakes. One unusual species breeds in pools of crude oil. The majority of larvae feed by filtering micro-organisms such as yeasts, bacteria and algae from the water. A few species feed in liquid manure, others on decaying plant or animal matter while some are miners of aquatic plant stems. The larvae of *Ochthera* species are predacious on other small, aquatic fly larvae. The adults of this strange genus have enlarged, raptorial front legs like mantids, and feed on small insects. *Notiphila*, *Hydrellia*, *Ephydra* and *Scatophila* are genera typical of the northern hemisphere.
**Economic importance** Species of *Hydrellia* can damage rice, watercress and other irrigated crops. Some species of *Ephydra* are so abundant along the shores of lakes that they have been collected and used by tribal peoples as food. In general, these flies are vital as part of the food chain for many waterbirds.

*Psilopa compta*

WS

# Lesser Fruit or Pomace Flies

**Order**  Diptera
**Family**  Drosophilidae
**Body length**  1–6mm (up to ¼in)
**Distribution**  Worldwide
**Number of species**  World–2900; NA–117; UK–52

**Identification**  These generally small flies are yellow, brown or black, usually shiny and have clear, darkly marked or entirely dark wings. The thorax is often marked with spots or stripes and the abdomen may also have patterns of bands or spots. A good recognition feature is the light or bright red eyes.
**Habitat**  Pomace flies can be found outside near rotting fruit, fermenting matter and in food and drink processing factories.
**Biology**  These flies are often called vinegar flies because of their attraction to fermenting products such as cider and spoiled wine. They are called lesser fruit flies to distinguish them from the Tephritidae. The eggs are laid in or near rotting fruit, decaying vegetation, sap flows and similar places. The whitish larvae have minute hook-like spines going all the way round each segment. The majority of larvae feed on bacteria, fungi and other micro-organisms but a few species are leaf-miners, and even fewer are parasites of the nymphs of homopteran bugs. More than half the total described species in this family belong to the genus *Drosophila*.
**Economic importance**  These flies can be a major pest in orchards and a nuisance in drinks factories, around cider presses and in the home. Despite this, they have been of immense help to science. Because of their small size, ease of culturing on artificial media, high reproduction rate and giant salivary chromosomes, they have been used for many years as laboratory insects in studies of genetics, cytology and physiology. Some species of *Drosophila* are the best-studied animals in the world and complete gene maps have been made.

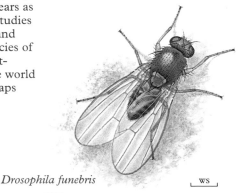

*Drosophila funebris*

WS

# Stem, Grass or Frit Flies

**Order** Diptera
**Family** Chloropidae
**Body length** 1–6mm (up to ¼in), mostly under 4mm (¼in)
**Distribution** Worldwide
**Number of species** World–2000; NA–280; UK–142

**Identification** Species of this large and common group of flies are grey, green or black with bright yellow markings. The body has very few obvious hairs or bristles and there is a clear, dark triangular plate on top of the head between the eyes which provides a good recognition feature for all members of the family. The abdomen is usually broad and tapers towards the hind end.

**Habitat** Adults can be found among rank vegetation, grasses, meadows, at decaying organic matter or at flowers.

**Biology** Adult chloropids may feed on nectar or other fluids. The larvae of most species are herbivorous, attacking cereals and grasses, while others may be saprophagous, feeding on insect frass or decaying plant material. Some species, such as those of *Lipara*, are gall-formers. Members of the genus *Thaumatomyia* are predacious on root aphids, and others eat the eggs of spiders, moths and other insects. Most of the genera represented in North America also occur across the northern hemisphere.

**Economic importance** There are several important pest species. *Oscinella frit* is a serious pest of wheat and other cereals on both sides of the Atlantic. The larvae bore into the young shoots and ears. Wheat stem maggots are larvae of *Meromyza* species which also cause the death of cereal ears. Some chloropids are attracted to body fluids around eyes, ears and other openings. They can be very annoying and in some parts of the world they transmit bacterial diseases, some of which can cause blindness.

*Oscinella frit*

WS

# Dung Flies

*Scatophaga stercoraria*

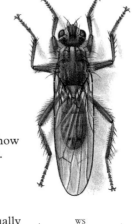

ws

**Order** Diptera
**Family** Scathophagidae
**Body length** 3–13mm (⅛–½in)
**Distribution** Northern hemisphere
**Number of species** World–250;
NA–148; UK–53

**Identification** Dung flies are black, yellow, grey or brown and sometimes show two of these colours in striking contrast. These flies may look superficially like house flies. The body may be sparsely hairy, but in general, the commonest species are very hairy or bristly, some looking almost furry. The wings are usually clear but may have darkish tinges or spots. The abdomen is slender but, in males, is enlarged at the rear end. The legs are slender and may have very strong dark bristles.

**Habitat** These flies are found mostly in the vicinity of fresh dung, although the less common species are found elsewhere.

**Biology** As far as is known, all adults are predacious on small insects. The eggs of some species are laid on orchids and lilies where the larvae are leaf-miners. Many species are herbivorous on a wide variety of plant species while others are predacious on small organisms in wet soil or water. In the commonest and best-known species, those of the genus *Scathophaga*, the eggs are laid in fresh cattle dung or in rodent burrows where the larvae are coprophagous. It may appear odd that members of the family are called dung flies when there are many not associated with dung. It is interesting to note that the name for this family is sometimes given as Scatophagidae but this name belongs to a family of butterfish. *Scathophaga stercoraria* is the Yellow Dung Fly, common across the northern hemisphere.

**Economic importance** Dung flies can sometimes be annoying around farmyards and certainly carry disease-producing organisms on their feet. They are, however, of no known significance.

# Anthomyiid Flies

**Order** Diptera
**Family** Anthomyiidae
**Body length** 2–12mm (⅛–½in), mostly 7–9mm (¼–⅜in)
**Distribution** Worldwide, mainly northern hemisphere
**Number of species** World–1500; NA–600; UK–225

**Identification** The anthomyiids comprise a large family of
rather ordinary-looking flies similar in general appearance to a
house fly although some may be bigger or smaller. The body
colour may be dull, yellowish-brown, grey, brown or black.
The slender, bristly legs are yellowish-brown or black. The
wings can be clear or with a smoky tinge.
**Habitat** The adults can be found in a wide range of terrestrial
habitats.
**Biology** The adults of many species feed on pollen and nectar
at umbelliferous and other flowers, while some species are
predacious on small insects. The larvae can be terrestrial or
semi-aquatic and show a wide range of feeding types.
Herbivorous species may be found as stem-borers, gall-formers
and leaf-miners in the roots, stems, flower heads and leaves of
a huge range of host plants. Saprophagous species can be
found in decaying organic matter, the excrement of birds and
animals and in rotting seaweed on the shore. A few species of
anthomyiids have larvae which live as inquilines or parasites in
the nests of solitary bees and wasps.
**Economic importance** A great many anthomyiids are
associated with cultivated plants and many are serious pests.
Many species have been accidentally introduced to North
America from Europe. Species of the genus *Pegomya* are
injurious to sugar beet, mangolds, spinach and raspberries
while species of *Hylemya* and *Delia* damage onion, turnip,
cabbage, carnations and wheat. Some are associated with
common weeds such as bracken (*Chirosia* spp.).

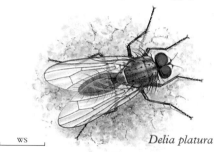

WS

*Delia platura*

# House Flies and their relatives

**Order** Diptera
**Family** Muscidae
**Body length** 2–12mm ($^1/_8$–$^1/_2$in)
**Distribution** Worldwide
**Number of species** World–3000; NA–622; UK–275

**Identification** This family of flies is a large and very variable group whose member species can be slender or stoutish and dull black, grey or yellowish in body coloration. The House Fly will be a familiar insect to everyone. All parts of the body usually have strong dark bristles and the legs are slender and quite long. The mouthparts act like a sponge for liquid foods. Blood-feeding species have piercing mouthparts.

**Habitats** Muscids are found on flowers, at excrement and decaying organic matter of all kinds. Blood-feeding species are associated with their hosts.

**Biology** Depending on species, adult muscids can be herbivorous, predacious, saprophagous, haematophagous or lick body fluids from large animals. The House Fly, *Musca domestica,* is typical of this family. Eggs are laid in masses in dung or any type of rotting organic matter. The maggot-like larvae develop fast and can pupate in just over a week. The larvae of other species may breed in fungi, birds nests, dry or wet soil, dead animals, water and inside plant tissues. The Stable Fly, *Stomoxys calcitrans,* will bite man and animals and is common around farm buildings. The larvae breed in rotting vegetable matter. There are many genera common across the northern hemisphere including *Phaonia, Spilogona* and *Mydaea.*

**Economic importance** Species that feed on the blood or body fluids of animals are serious pests and vectors for many parasitic diseases of man and animals. As many adult muscids make contact with excrement and other rotting matter, they can transfer a huge variety of bacterial, viral, protozoal and worm infections via their feet and mouthparts. Among the diseases known to be spread by these flies are cholera, typhoid, poliomyelitis and dysentery.

*Musca domestica*

WS

# Blow Flies

**Order** Diptera
**Family** Calliphoridae
**Body length**
4–16mm (¼–⅝in),
mostly 7–12mm (¼–½in)
**Distribution** Worldwide
**Number of species**
World–1200; NA–80;
UK–33

*Calliphora
vomitoria*

WS

**Identification** Calliphorids
are generally stout-bodied
flies with metallic green or
blue, shiny black or dull
coloration and few bristles.
They are similar in
appearance to sarcophagids and tachinids and are usually the
same size or bigger than a house fly. The tips of the antennae
are distinctively feathered. In some species, the sexes are of
different colours.
**Habitat** Adults can be found on flowers, vegetation, close to
animal carcasses and excrement or indoors where they are
attracted to fresh or cooked meats, fish and dairy produce.
**Biology** Typical species, often called blue bottles or green
bottles, belong to the genera *Calliphora* and *Lucilia*
respectively. The adults feed on pollen, nectar and a range of
rotting animal and plant matter. Calliphorid eggs are laid in
carrion and dung or on flesh. The larvae are saprophagous or
flesh-eaters. The cosmopolitan species *Lucilia caesar* breeds in
carcasses and dung while the sheep maggot fly, *L. sericata*, lays
eggs on the wool of sheep and the hatched larvae burrow into
the flesh. The cluster flies of the genus *Pollenia* lay their eggs in
the soil and the larvae attack worms. These flies often
hibernate in attics in large numbers. Larvae of the genus
*Protocalliphora* suck the blood of nestling birds.
**Economic importance** Many species in this family are of
considerable medical and veterinary importance. The flesh-
eating larvae of many species can infest livestock and in some
cases, humans. *Cochliomyia hominvorax*, the Cattle Screw
Worm, is a serious pest in the Americas but has been largely
eradicated from North America by sterile male release
programmes. Many calliphorids carry enteric diseases such as
dysentery, for they are attracted to excrement and foodstuffs.

# Flesh Flies

**Order** Diptera
**Family** Sarcophagidae
**Body length** 2–20mm (⅛–¾in), mostly 6–10mm (¼–⅜in)
**Distribution** Worldwide, mainly northern hemisphere
**Number of species** World–2100; NA–330; UK–55

**Identification** These robust flies are mostly dull grey or black and are never metallic. The body hairs are yellowish but the most distinctive features are the longitudinally striped thorax and the chequered or marbled abdominal patterns. The abdominal pattern seems to change from light to dark depending on the viewing angle. The sexes sometimes have different body colour.

**Habitat** Sarcophagids are found in a variety of habitats but the adults are frequently seen feeding on nectar at flowers, at sap flowing from tree wounds and on aphid honeydew.

**Biology** Adult female sarcophagids give birth to larvae not eggs. The eggs develop and hatch internally and the white or yellow, cylindrical, anteriorally tapering larvae are laid or dropped from the air on the appropriate substrate. The range of larval habits in this family is quite diverse. Many are carrion-feeders, some are parasites of other insects such as beetles, grasshoppers and the caterpillars of butterflies and moths, while others parasitize vertebrates like turtles, frogs, chameleons as well as less exotic, wild and domestic animals. In some unusual sarcophagids, the larvae live in the nests of ground-living wasps or bees where they eat the provisions left for the young. Still stranger are the sarcophagids that live in the insect-trapping leaves of pitcher plants. Species of the genus *Sarcophaga* are common and widespread, some being cosmopolitan.

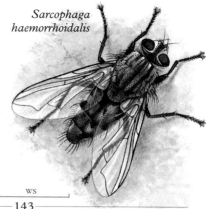

*Sarcophaga haemorrhoidalis*

**Economic importance** Flesh flies are not as important pests as the calliphorids but there have been cases of larvae burrowing into the soft skin of human infants. Serious intestinal problems can result from eating food containing eggs or larvae. Some species are used to control insect pests.

WS

# Parasitic Flies

**Order** Diptera
**Family** Tachinidae
**Body length** 5–15mm (¼–⅝in)
**Distribution** Worldwide
**Number of species** World–7800; NA–1280; UK–235

**Identification** Members of this very large family of stout-bodied flies exhibit a huge range of body colour and patterns, from pale or dark brown to black, reddish or metallic green. The thorax and abdomen may be plain or with stripes, spots or bands of contrasting colours. The majority of species largely resemble bristly house flies but some can be much larger, very hairy and almost bee-like. The abdomen is especially well provided with stout, erect bristles, particularly on the rear half and around the margins. The wings are usually clear but some species have spotted or dark wings.
**Habitat** Tachinids are found virtually everywhere. The adults are often seen at flowers, at tree sap or on honeydew.
**Biology** The adults feed on carbohydrate-rich food sources, especially honeydew. They are very active indeed and hard to catch. Males of many species congregate on hilltops, waiting for receptive females. The larvae of tachinids are all parasitic on other insects. There are a variety of ways in which the hosts can be parasitized. The eggs can be laid directly on or inside the host's body, eaten with food material or, in some cases, the tachinid female lays directly into the mouth of the host insect while it is feeding. The range of insect hosts used by these flies is extensive and includes the adult and immature stages of Lepidoptera, Coleoptera, Orthoptera, Hemiptera, Hymenoptera, Diptera and some other orders. The larvae eat and eventually kill the host, obtaining air from the outside through a hole in the host's body or by 'plugging in' to a trachea. There are very many genera common to both sides of the Atlantic.
**Economic importance** These flies are of great importance in the control of natural populations of pest insects. Many species have been used or are under investigation as biological control agents.

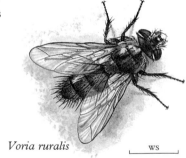

*Voria ruralis*

WS

# Bot and Warble Flies

*Oestris ovis*

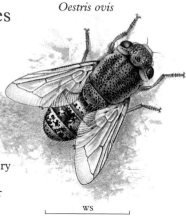

**Order** Diptera
**Family** Oestridae
**Body length** 8–25mm (³⁄₈–1in), mostly under 18mm (³⁄₄in)
**Distribution** Nearly worldwide
**Number of species** World–160; NA–41; UK–10

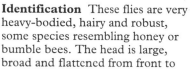

ws

**Identification** These flies are very heavy-bodied, hairy and robust, some species resembling honey or bumble bees. The head is large, broad and flattened from front to back. The antennae are small and partly contained in grooves on the head. The mouthparts are very small or absent. The abdomen can be rounded or conical and shiny, often with a dense covering of hairs. The ovipositor of the females is long and extensible. The body surface of some species is warty or wrinkled in appearance. The legs are short, stout and hairy.

**Habitat** The males of some species congregate on hilltops for mating purposes. Females can be found close to their mammalian hosts.

**Biology** The majority of adult oestrids do not feed at all. The larvae are all parasites of mammals and the species are very host-specific. Eggs are usually laid on the hair of the host, although in some cases larvae are laid into the nostrils of the host, the eggs having first hatched inside the body of the female fly. The horse bot flies (subfamily: Gasterophilinae) include *Gasterophilus haemorrhoidalis* and related species. The eggs are laid on the shoulders and legs and ingested as the horse licks. The larvae develop in the rectum, stomach or intestines and pass out of the horse to pupate on the ground. The Oestridae contains the Sheep Bot Fly (*Oestrus ovis*) and other species that parasitize deer and horses by way of the nasal passages. The warble flies (subfamily: Hypodermatinae) attack cattle and deer, their larvae entering by the legs and burrowing under the skin to the animal's back where large swellings or 'warbles' develop. The mature larvae chew their way out and pupate in soil. In other parts of the world, species in this family attack a wide range of animals.

**Economic importance** Many species are serious pests of wild and domestic livestock and sometimes humans.

# Louse Flies

**Order** Diptera
**Family** Hippoboscidae
**Body length** 1.5–12mm (⅛–½in), mostly 4–7mm (¼–⅜in)
**Distribution** Worldwide
**Number of species** World–200; NA–30; UK–10

**Identification** These strange-looking, ectoparasitic flies are
stout, tough-bodied, hairy, flattened and usually dull-coloured
with pale markings. The broad and flattened head is usually
partly sunk into the thorax and the mouthparts, which form a
piercing proboscis, point forwards. The eyes are rounded or
oval and the antennae are short and sunk into a depression of
the head. Many species have reduced wings or are wingless.
Fully winged species lose their wings once a host is located.
The claws of the legs are strong and modified for holding on to
the hair or feathers of the host animal.
**Habitat** Hippoboscids are found on the body of their avian or
mammalian hosts.
**Biology** The females do not lay eggs but instead produce
mature larvae which have developed inside a uterus and have
been nourished on the secretions of special milk glands. In
most cases, only one larva is produced per year. Some species
mate only once in their lifetime while others may mate
repeatedly. The larva pupate almost immediately on their
host's fur, feathers or nests. The adults are all blood-suckers
and mostly host-specific, although some species can parasitize
a small range of related hosts. Species of the genus
*Ornithomyia* are ectoparasites of birds. The dark brown and
wingless Sheep Ked, *Melophagus ovinus*, is cosmopolitan in
distribution. The mature
larvae attach themselves to
the wool using a special
glue and pupate within 12
hours. The adults that
emerge remain on the
sheep, sucking blood.
Species of the genus
*Hippobosca* parasitize cattle,
horses and deer.
**Economic importance**
Species attacking domestic
animals are of significant
economic importance.

*Melophagus
ovinus*

BL

146

# Purse Casemaker or Micro Caddisflies

**Order** Trichoptera
**Family** Hydroptilidae
**Body length**
2–6mm (⅛–¼in)
**Distribution** Worldwide
**Number of species** World–1000;
NA–200; UK–29

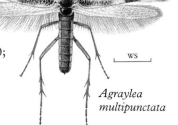

*Agraylea
multipunctata*

**Identification** These small
caddisflies have a black, white or
grey, speckled coloration and
sometimes have pale yellowish
tinges. The antennae are relatively short. The body is densely
covered with hairs and the wings, which are long and narrow,
have fringes of hairs around their margins longer than the
width of the wings. The wing hairs are sometimes club-ended.
At rest, the wings are folded together flat over the body like
moth wings. In flight, the wings are coupled by rows of hook-
like hairs projecting from the leading edge of the hind wings.
**Habitat** Many species are common and widely distributed,
occurring near rivers and lakes.
**Biology** As with most caddisflies, the adults do not feed, and
at certain times of the year large mating swarms can be seen.
Eggs are laid in jelly-like masses on the water or on marginal
vegetation. The first four larval stages have a short abdomen
and, in addition to the thoracic legs, have longish abdominal
prolegs. They are active and free-living in the water, sucking
the juices of water plants such as *Spirogyra* through modified
mouthparts. The larvae do not have special requirements in
terms of water temperature, current or bottom substrate and
can be found in the flowing or standing water of ponds or
streams. The last larval stage has a swollen abdomen and
makes an open-ended purse or barrel-shaped case of silk, often
with small stones attached. Pupation takes place in the case
and the adult emerges from the pupal skin at the water's
surface. Species of *Agraylea*, *Hydroptila* and *Oxyethira* are
common across the northern hemisphere.
**Economic importance** Micro caddisflies are of no
significant importance.

# Northern Caddisflies

**Order** Trichoptera
**Family** Limnephilidae
**Body length** 7–30mm (¼–1¼in), mostly under 24mm (1in)
**Distribution** Primarily northern hemisphere
**Number of species** World–1500; NA–310; UK–54

**Identification** Species of this, the largest family of caddisflies, are very northern in distribution. Adults are quite large with a generally pale reddish, yellowish or dark brownish coloration and often have fine, irregular, dark wing markings. The front wings are narrow, paper-like, have very few hairs and appear abruptly cut off at their ends. The hind wings are broad and fairly transparent. At rest, the wings are held roof-like over the body. The antennae are about as long as the front wings.
**Habitat** These caddisflies are common and widespread around ponds, streams and lakes of all sizes. Some breed in ditches and marshy places.
**Biology** The omnivorous larvae can be found in a wide variety of habitats and have variable preferences in terms of water current, temperature and substrate texture. They make tubular cases of all kinds of materials including sand grains, pebbles, vegetation, sticks and shells or mixtures of materials. In species that exclusively use twigs, the cases are known as log cabins. Some larvae incorporate larger twigs in the case to prevent fish from swallowing them. In some species, the cases made by the younger stages can be of a different design from those made by the older stages. *Limnephilus* is a very large and widespread genus.
**Economic importance** Limnephilids are of no significant economic importance.

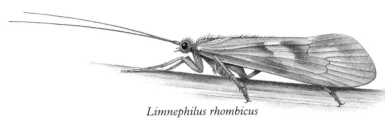

*Limnephilus rhombicus*

ws

# Giant Casemaker or Large Caddisflies

**Order** Trichoptera
**Family** Phryganeidae
**Body length** 12–26mm (½–1in)
**Distribution** Northern hemisphere
**Number of species** World–500; NA–26; UK–10

**Identification** Phryganeids are irregularly marked with light brown or grey and often have a mottled appearance. The wings of some species can be quite brightly marked with black or orange or have dark margins and stripes. The antennae are relatively short, in some species – just about as long as the front wings.
**Habitat** These caddisflies are found near ponds and marshes.
**Biology** The larvae are predacious on small aquatic animals and, as a result, need a strong but light case which can be easily moved around. The beautifully regular, tapering cases are silk-lined and made of spirally arranged plant fragments and fibres with the occasional bit of gravel incorporated. The larvae prefer the slow-moving or static, cold water of marshes or eddies and a silty substrate with plenty of plant debris. The pieces of plant fragment or stem used for the cases are of exact dimensions, being measured by the larva against the front part of its body. Species of *Agrypnia* and *Phryganea* are common.
**Economic importance** Large caddisflies are of no significant economic importance.

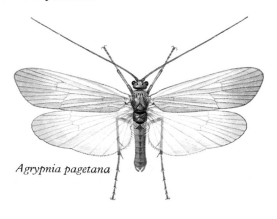

*Agrypnia pagetana*

ws

# Goat or Carpenter Moths

**Order** Lepidoptera
**Family** Cossidae
**Wingspan** 20–75mm (¾–3in)
**Distribution** Worldwide
**Number of species** World–1000; NA–45; UK–3

**Identification** These medium or large-sized moths are heavy-bodied and usually have spotted, irregularly patterned or mottled wings. The wingspan can be up to 180mm (7in) in some species but is rarely over 75mm (3in) in northern hemisphere species. The antennae are often comb-like on both sides and in both sexes. The mouthparts or proboscis are reduced and sometimes very rudimentary. They look superficially like hawk moths and are good fliers.
**Habitat** In the northern hemisphere, these moths inhabit deciduous forests and are particularly associated with oak, poplar, chestnut and willow trees.
**Biology** The adults are nocturnal and rarely feed. Females may lay thousands of eggs in the course of their lives. The eggs are laid in tree or shrub bark fissures or in the adult emergence tunnels. A few species bore in the pith of reeds. The larvae feed internally in the wood, producing large tunnels and taking many years to reach adulthood. When fully grown, the larvae pupate in their tunnels or in the soil, in a cocoon made of silk and chewed wood fibres. The name goat moth is derived from the fact that the larvae of many species produce a strong and sometimes unpleasant odour. The Leopard Moth, *Zeuzera pyrina*, was introduced to North America from Europe. The larvae bore in the wood of various shrubs and trees. *Cossus cossus* is the European Goat Moth.
**Economic importance** Several species are pests of commercially important trees. In Australia, where there are many species in this family, arboriginal people eat witchety grubs, which are the mature larvae of some cossid species.

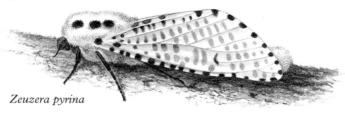

*Zeuzera pyrina*

ws

# Tortricid Moths

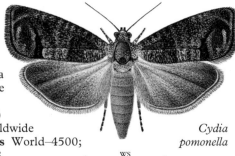

**Order** Lepidoptera
**Family** Tortricidae
**Wingspan**
8–34mm (³/₈–1³/₈in)
**Distribution** Worldwide
**Number of species** World–4500;
NA–1060; UK–308

*Cydia pomonella*

ws

**Identification** Species of this large family of smallish moths are brown, green or greyish in colour and exhibit a multitude of cryptic patterns resembling bark, lichen, bird droppings and bits of leaves. The hind wings are usually more or less uniform grey or brown. Some species are brightly coloured and may have metallic spots. The front wings are broadly rectangular and square-ended in most species. The wings are held roof-like over the body at rest and, in some species, make a bell shape (bell moths). The head is covered with rough scales. The females of some species have vestigial wings.

**Habitat** Tortricids are found virtually everywhere.

**Biology** The caterpillars are herbivorous and feed in leaf litter, between leaves that they tie or roll together with silk. Other species bore into fruit, stems and leaves and a few make galls. Tortricids may be monophagous, oligophagous or polyphagous depending on species. As a family, they attack a huge range of plant species. *Eucosma*, *Epinotia*, *Olethreutes* and *Acleris* are just a few of the genera common across the northern hemisphere. The seed-feeding larvae of *Cydia saltitans* live inside the seed of croton plants in Mexico and Arizona. The violent wriggling of these caterpillars has given rise to the story of strange jumping beans.

**Economic importance** There are very many pest species in this large family, attacking and damaging a huge range of commercially important trees and soft fruit crops. About one third of all tortricid genera contain pest species. *Cydia pomonella*, the Codling Moth, was introduced to North America over 200 years ago and is a serious pest of apples. Notwith-standing the general unease of eating a 'wormy' apple, the presence of a moth larva at least shows that the fruit is free from pesticide residues. Some weed-feeding tortricids have been used as biological control agents.

# Clothes Moths and their relatives

**Order** Lepidoptera
**Family** Tineidae
**Wingspan** 8–20mm (³⁄₈–³⁄₄in), mostly under 15mm (⁵⁄₈in)
**Distribution** Worldwide
**Number of species** World–2500; NA–180; UK–47

**Identification** People will be more familiar with the effects of clothes moths than with the moths themselves. Adults are usually drab and plainly coloured, many being dull brown. The head has a covering of raised, hair-like scales or bristles. The antennae are usually simple with whorls of scales on each segment but can appear toothed or comb-like in some species. The proboscis is short or absent. The front wings are quite narrow and are held at a steep angle over the body at rest. Many species will not fly readily and prefer to run rapidly, using their long legs.
**Habitat** Tineids can be found outside around rotting wood, fungi and dried organic matter in a variety of habitats or indoors on fur, woollen fabrics, textiles and dry foodstuffs.
**Biology** The caterpillars of these moths are scavengers and feed in fungi, rotting wood, dried fruit, grain and a huge range of dry plant and animal matter. Very few species feed on plant foliage. Some species make portable cases of silk and debris and others produce a web of silk wherever they feed.
**Economic importance** Many species are pests and several have a cosmopolitan distribution. The Webbing Clothes Moth, *Tineola bisselliella*, the Tapestry Moth, *Trichophaga tapetzella*, and the Case Bearing Clothes Moth, *Tinea pellionella*, are among the most damaging of household pest insects, destroying clothes, carpets, furs, woollens and silks.

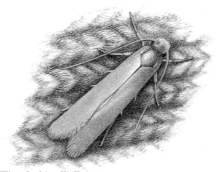

*Tineola bisselliella*  ∟ ws ⌐

# Leaf Blotch-mining Moths

**Order** Lepidoptera
**Family** Gracillariidae
**Wingspan** 4–22mm (¼–¾in), mostly under 15mm (⅝in)
**Distribution** Worldwide
**Number of species** World–1200; NA–280; UK–80

**Identification** These small moths are usually brightly coloured yellow and brown with distinct markings. They have long, narrow front wings and very slender, pointed hind wings. Both pairs of wings have long fringes of hairs, especially on the hind margins. The head is covered with smooth scales and the antennae are as long or longer than the length of the front wings. In the field, they are recognizable by the way they rest with their bodies raised on the front and middle pairs of legs.
**Habitat** Gracillariids are primarily woodland moths.
**Biology** The adults fly rapidly at dawn or dusk and spend the day resting on tree trunks. The caterpillars are herbivorous, mining or skeletonizing leaves of a wide range of trees and shrubs. Most species make silk-lined, blotch mines (a few make serpentine mines) between the upper and lower leaf epidermis of their host plants. When young, the caterpillars have small mouthparts and can only break open cells and suck the contents. When older, they can chew the mesophyll cells. Some species make a mine when young and then roll the edges of the leaves. The fully grown caterpillars pupate in the mine or in a leaf roll. Species of the genera *Caloptilia* and *Phyllonorycter* are common and widespread.
**Economic importance** A few gracillariids are of economic importance and cause damage to commercial and ornamental tree species.

*Caloptilia stigmatella*

ws

# Clearwings or Clear-winged Moths

**Order** Lepidoptera
**Family** Sesiidae
**Wingspan** 14–40mm (⅝–1⅝in)
**Distribution** Worldwide
**Number of species** World–1000; NA–120; UK–15

**Identification** Clear-winged moths are very brightly coloured black, bluish or dark brown with yellow and orange markings and many resemble wasps or bees. Large areas of the wings are clear, scales being present only along the veins. The front wings are long and narrow with rounded ends and the hind wings, which have larger clear areas, are broader. The antennae often have expanded ends. The abdomen is often banded and may bear a fan-shaped tuft of scale-like hairs.
**Habitat** The adults fly during the day and can be seen around flowers or near their host plants in a variety of habitats.
**Biology** The mimicry of wasps and bees shown by these moths is emphasized by their buzzing flight. Some species may even pretend to sting. The eggs are generally laid on the trunks or stems of trees and shrubs and the caterpillars bore their way inside. The caterpillars of some species may also damage roots. The caterpillars take two years to develop, and when mature, they spend the winter in their tunnels. In many species, the wings are fully scaled when the moths emerge from their pupae, the scales being shed during the first flight. Species of the genera *Sesia* and *Synanthedon* are common. *Sesia apiformis* is the Hornet Clearwing Moth whose caterpillars damage the trunks and roots of poplar and willow trees.
**Economic importance** Many species are pests of orchard and other useful trees and shrubs. *Synanthedon excitosa*, the PeachTree Borer of North America, is found everywhere that peaches are grown.

*Sesia apiformis*

ws

# Diamondback Moths

**Order** Lepidoptera
**Family** Plutellidae
**Wingspan** 10–22mm (³⁄₈–³⁄₄in)
**Distribution** Nearly worldwide
**Number of species** World–380; NA–52; UK–19

**Identification** Plutellids are cryptically or drably coloured grey or brown and many have dark and light bands or irregular markings. The front wings are long and narrow with broadly rounded ends and marginal fringes of hair. The hind wings are much broader with longer hair fringes, especially on the hind edge. When the wings are folded over the body at rest, many species appear to have a row of diamond-shaped marks running from front to back.

**Habitat** These moths can be found in a variety of habitats and are commonly found in the vicinity of their host plants.

**Biology** The caterpillars are herbivorous on a range of trees, shrubs and plants. They feed externally on foliage within a flimsy web or mine leaves and stems. *Plutella xylostella*, the Diamondback Moth, is a typical species. The greenish-brown caterpillars eat crucifers and brassicas. The family is sometimes regarded as a subfamily of the closely related Yponomeutidae. The genera *Plutella* and *Ypsolopha* contain many common and widespread species. Some species are cosmopolitan.

**Economic importance** Many species are common vegetable crop pests and their range has become greatly increased through trade.

*Plutella maculipennis*

WS

# Casebearing or Sac Moths

**Order** Lepidoptera
**Family** Coleophoridae
**Wingspan** 7–15mm (¼–⅝in), mostly 12mm (½in)
**Distribution** Worldwide, mainly northern hemisphere
**Number of species** World–800; NA–168; UK–101

**Identification** These common, small moths are plain brown
or grey and may have pale stripes on the front wings. They can
be easily recognized by the way they hold their antennae
stretched out when at rest. The head has smooth scales and
the hind legs have rough, scale-like hairs. The front wings are
narrow and pointed with a hair fringe at the ends and on the
hind margin. The hind wings are very narrow indeed and have
fringes of very long hairs.
**Habitat** Coleophorids are woodland species but some occur
in damp meadows.
**Biology** The caterpillars are phytophagous on a wide range of
trees, shrubs and herbaceous plants. When young, the
caterpillars feed externally or mine leaves. As they get older,
each species makes a distinctive case from bits of its host plant.
The small cases may be pistol, cigar, oval or irregularly shaped
and held together with silk. Coleophorids lay their eggs in
summer and the caterpillars usually overwinter inside their
cases to resume feeding in the spring. The only major genus in
this family is *Coleophora* with 550 species in the northern
hemisphere. The vast majority of coleophorid species in North
America and Britain belong to this genus.
**Economic importance** Several species are of economic
interest, including *Coleophora serratella*, the Cigar Casebearer,
whose caterpillars attack birch, apple and other fruit trees.
Some species are pests of larch and other commercial trees.

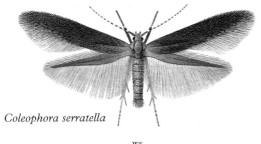

*Coleophora serratella*

WS

# Oecophorid Moths

**Order** Lepidoptera
**Family** Oecophoridae
**Wingspan** 8–29mm (³⁄₈–1¼in)
**Distribution** Worldwide
**Number of species** World–3500; NA–230; UK–80

**Identification** Oecophorids are small, somewhat flattened moths which may be brownish, yellowish, black and white and with dull markings or with very bright, gold, metallic or other markings. The shape of the front wings is variable, normally broadish and with rounded ends but in some species, narrow and pointed. The hind wings are generally broader than the front wings.

**Habitat** These moths can be found in a variety of wooded and open habitats in association with their host plants. A very few species can be found indoors.

**Biology** The caterpillars of many species are poorly known. Of the known species, caterpillars are herbivorous or fungus-feeders and some may be saprophagous. A few species eat lichens and scavenge in decaying wood. The caterpillars of a typical plant-feeding species, *Depressaria pastinacella,* the Parsnip Webworm, tie up the heads of umbelliferous flowers like parsnip, wild carrot and related plants with silk. The grey, black-spotted caterpillars feed inside the silk web and then burrow down the stems.

**Economic Importance** Relatively few oecophorids are of economic importance but the Brown House Moth, *Hofmannophila pseudospretella,* is worth a mention. The caterpillars of this minor household pest, originally imported to North America from Europe, feed on a wide range of stored products and will also attack woollens, furs and linen. When not in houses, the caterpillars feed in the nests of birds.

*Agonopterix heracliana*

ws

# Gelechiid Moths

**Order** Lepidoptera
**Family** Gelechiidae
**Wingspan** 7–27mm (³⁄₈–1¹⁄₈in)
**Distribution** Worldwide
**Number of species** World–4200; NA–635; UK–145

**Identification** Gelechiids are small or very small moths, together comprising one of the largest families of microlepidoptera. They are predominantly grey or brown and are often overlooked. The head is covered with smooth scales and the hind tibiae have long hair-like scales. The front wings can be narrowly rounded or pointed at their ends. The hind wings provide a good recognition feature in that the apex is long, acute and points forward. The rear margin of the hind wings is sinuate or concave in outline.

**Habitat** These moths can be found in a large range of habitats and can be seen flying at dusk near their food plants.

**Biology** The caterpillars are phytophagous and feed externally, although some species may be leaf-rollers, leaf-tiers, leaf-miners or gall-formers. Caterpillars spin shelters of silk in the leaves, shoots or flower heads of their host plants and feed inside. Some species may burrow down stems or eat seeds.

**Economic importance** Many species are serious pests and a great variety of crops including potato, tomato, aubergine, peanuts, strawberries, soft fruit trees and commercial softwood trees can suffer great damage. The caterpillars of the cosmopolitan Angoumois Grain Moth, *Sitotroga cerealella*, feed in the kernels of corn and stored grain. The pantropical, Pink Boll Worm, *Pectinophora gossypiella*, is a very destructive cotton pest, whose caterpillars feed on the pollen and soft parts of the cotton flowers.

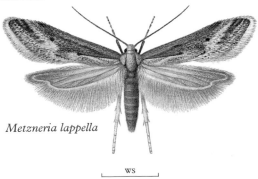

*Metzneria lappella*

ws

# Pyralid, Snout or Grass Moths

**Order** Lepidoptera
**Family** Pyralidae
**Wingspan** 10–40mm (³⁄₈–1⁵⁄₈in)
**Distribution** Worldwide
except New Zealand
**Number of species**
World–17,500; NA–1380;
UK–165

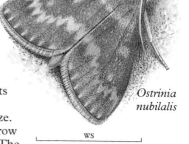

*Ostrinia
nubilalis*

ws

**Identification** This family of
moths is very large indeed and its
member species exhibit a huge
diversity of colour, shape and size.
The wings may be broad or narrow
and have closely packed scales. The
front wings are usually oblong or triangular and the hind wings
are broad and rounded. In some species the front of the head
looks as if it has a small snout. The 'snout' is formed by the
palps of the mouthparts being elongate and held out straight.
The proboscis is scale-covered. The antennae are simple and
thread-like. The legs are long.
**Habitat** The species in this family occur everywhere.
**Biology** The caterpillars are mainly phytophagous, boring
into the stems and roots or feeding externally and rolling and
tying the leaves of their host plants. Other pyralids are
scavengers, a few are carnivorous and a few are aquatic, boring
in the roots of submerged plants. There are a great number of
genera common to both sides of the Atlantic.
**Economic importance** A very large number of species are
pests. The list of crops and dry, stored products damaged by
these micromoths is endless. In North America, a list of crops
would include cabbage, grasses, beet, alfalfa, cucumber,
sweetcorn, apple, sunflower, plum, tobacco and many others.
One of the most important pests is the European Corn Borer,
*Ostrinia nubilalis,* whose caterpillars damage young corn. This
species was introduced by accident to North America early this
century. *Galleria mellonella* is the Wax Moth, whose caterpillars
have special enzymes for digesting honeycomb. The Meal
Moth, *Pyralis farinalis,* is a pest in stored grain.

# Skippers

**Order** Lepidoptera
**Family** Hesperiidae
**Wingspan** 20–65mm (¾–2½in), most under 40mm (1⅝in)
**Distribution** Worldwide except New Zealand
**Number of species** World–3500; NA–300; UK–8

**Identification** The skippers form a group which are closely related to, but distinct from, the butterflies. They have many easily recognizable features. In general, they are moth-like, very heavy-bodied. The head is as wide as the thorax. Many of them are drably coloured, brown with white or orange markings. A few are predominantly pale or have blue, green or purplish tinges. The antennae are widely separated at their bases and end in an elongated club which comes to a point and is often curved back on itself. The wings look small in comparison to the heavy body and, in some species the hind wings are prolonged as tails. At rest the wings can be held upright butterfly-style or folded back like those of moths.
**Habitat** Skippers are common in a variety of habitats where their host plants occur.
**Biology** The common name comes from their rapid, darting flight pattern. The phytophagous caterpillars have a large head with a constricted neck region, and are smooth and taper towards the rear end. They eat grasses and the foliage of some trees and herbaceous plants and usually live within a shelter of silk-tied or rolled leaves. When fully grown, they pupate at the base of the host plant inside a silken web which often has bits of plant incorporated. *Thymelicus lineola*, the European Skipper, has been introduced to North America. This species lives in meadows where its caterpillars feed on grass species.
**Economic importance**
In addition to a few of the grass-feeders, several species feed on leguminous plants and can be minor pests.

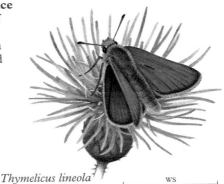

*Thymelicus lineola*

ws

# Swallowtails and Apollos

**Order** Lepidoptera
**Family** Papilionidae
**Wingspan** 50–125mm (2–4⅞in)
**Distribution** Worldwide, primarily warm regions
**Number of species** World–700; NA–35; UK–1

**Identification** These butterflies are often large and can be spectacularly attractive. The swallowtails (Papilioninae) have a black ground colour marked with bands, spots or patches of yellow, orange, red, green or blue. They have short or long tails directed backwards from the ends of the hind wings. In some species the ends of the tails are broad with coloured centres. The apollos (Parnassiinae) do not have hind wing tails and are translucent white or grey in general colour often with two reddish or yellowish spots on each hind wing. All pairs of legs in members of this family are functional.

**Habitat** Apollos are generally mountain-dwellers and swallowtails can be found in a variety of flower-rich areas.

**Biology** Caterpillars are herbivorous on trees and herbaceous plants across a variety of plant familes. The adults and their caterpillars are usually distasteful to predators and a characteristic feature of the caterpillars is the possession of a strange, forked, thoracic scent gland which can be everted. The gland, called the osmeterium, is brightly coloured and gives off an unpleasant odour. The caterpillars may also be spiny or with fleshy, warty protuberances. The chrysalis is upright and held in place by a silk belt. Apollos pupate on the ground among plant litter in loosely woven cocoons. *Papilio* species are swallowtails, *Parnassius* species are apollos.

**Economic importance**
These butterflies are of great aesthetic value.

*Papilio machaon*

ws

# White, Sulphur and Orange Tip Butterflies

**Order** Lepidoptera
**Family** Pieridae
**Wingspan** 20–70mm (¾–2¾in)
**Distribution** Worldwide
**Number of species** World–1300; NA–65; UK–10

**Identification** The species that comprise this family are among the commonest butterflies anywhere in the world. The wings of these butterflies are usually white, yellow or orange with black or dark grey markings and spots. There is often a clear difference in coloration between the sexes. The legs are of normal development and the hind margin of the hind wings appears convex.

**Habitat** Pierids can be found in a huge range of habitats ranging from open meadows to woodlands and from mountainous areas to sea level.

**Biology** The adults are day-flying and can often be seen in groups at puddles in warm sunshine after rain. Some species migrate and often in large numbers. The caterpillars are very uniform in appearance, being smooth, elongate and having no projections or spines. Some are slightly hairy and although many are coloured to match the background, some may have aposematic colours. Larval food plants are commonly legumes, crucifers or brassicas. The angular, elongate pupae have a distinctive single spiny projection from the head end and are attached upright to the host plant by a silk belt. The genera *Euchloe*, *Synchloe* (orange tips), *Colias* (clouded yellows) and *Gonepteryx* (brimstones) are typical of the northern hemisphere.

**Economic importance** Many species are pests around the world. *Pieris brassicae* and *P. rapae* are pests of brassica crops, the latter species being one of the most damaging of all butterfly species. Many species of herbaceous legumes and cruciferous crops are damaged by the Pieridae.

*Pieris rapae*

WS

# Fritillaries, Admirals, Emperors and Tortoiseshells

**Order** Lepidoptera
**Family** Nymphalidae
**Wingspan** 30–110mm (1¼–4⅜in), mostly 40–80mm (1⅝–3¼in)
**Distribution** Worldwide
**Number of species** World–3500; NA–140; UK–18

**Identification** The species that comprise this butterfly family are common. The wings are usually very brightly coloured and marked on the upper surfaces but usually dull and cryptically coloured on the under surfaces. In North America, they are called brush foots because the front legs are very small and not used for walking. The female's front legs, although small, may have a sensory function in the location of host plants.
**Habitat** Nymphalids can be found everywhere but especially in flower-rich meadows and woodland clearings.
**Biology** Adult females lay ribbed eggs on a huge variety of trees, shrubs and herbaceous plants. The caterpillars are generally spiny and may have horn-like projections at either end of the body. The angular pupae, which often have gold or silver spots and prominent, warty tubercles, are suspended head down from the host plant by a small group of terminal hooks called the cremaster. The Painted Lady, *Vanessa cardui*, is a noted migratory species. The caterpillars feed on nettles, thistles, sunflowers and other plants. *Vanessa atalanta*, the Red Admiral, and *Nymphalis antiopa*, the Mourning Cloak, also occur on both sides of the Atlantic.
**Economic importance** No nymphalids are pest species.

*Vanessa cardui*

WS

# Nymphs, Arctics, Satyrs and Ringlets

**Order** Lepidoptera
**Family** Satyridae
**Wingspan** 28–74mm (1¼–3in)
**Distribution** Worldwide, mainly temperate regions
**Number of species** World–2000; NA–50; UK–11

**Identification** Satyrids are pale yellowish-brown to dark brown or greyish coloured butterflies and often have numerous eyespots around the wing margins. The eyespots are commonly dark-ringed, white spots surrounded by a colour paler than the wing colour. A characteristic feature of this family is the pronounced swelling of several veins near the bases of the wings. The sexes are very similar but the females may be a little larger and paler than the males. As in the Nymphalidae and the Danaidae, the front pair of legs is very reduced and not used for walking.
**Habitat** These butterflies are shade lovers and can be found in heath, open meadows and light woodland of upland areas.
**Biology** The adults are not very good fliers but when they do fly, they fly in a characteristic, erratic and bobbing manner. The caterpillars of all species are grass- or sedge-feeders. They are brown, yellow or green with very small warts bearing short hairs and often have longitudinal pale stripes. An easily recognizable feature of the caterpillars is the forked tail segment. The pupae are similar to those of the Nymphalidae but have no obvious ridges or tubercles. The pupae either hang upside down from the host plant or lie on the ground in an insubstantial cocoon. The genus *Erebia* is typical of the European Alps and the mountains of Asia and North America. The majority of North American satyrid species are found in the north or mountains of the west. Some authors have considered the Satyridae as a subfamily of the Nymphalidae.
**Economic importance** Satyrids are of no economic importance.

*Coenonympha tullia*

ws

# Milkweed Butterflies

**Order** Lepidoptera
**Family** Danaidae
**Wingspan** 60–100mm (2⅜–4in)
**Distribution** Worldwide, primarily warmer regions
**Number of species** World–300; NA–4; UK–1

**Identification** The best-known species are blackish-brown and reddish-orange with small white marks, although some species may have brown, green or yellow coloration. Danaids are large and, like the nymphalids and satyrids, have non-functional front legs, which, in females, end in ridged, knob-like structures. The antennae are not covered with scales.
**Habitat** Danaids can be found in flower-rich, open areas where milkweeds and other host plants occur.
**Biology** The American Monarch Butterfly, *Danaus plexippus*, which sometimes reaches the shores of Europe as a vagrant, is typical. The adults and caterpillars are highly distasteful to predators on account of the toxic compounds they obtain from their host plants and store in their bodies. The host plants are of the family Asclepiadaceae and contain cardiac glycosides, poisonous to vertebrates. The coloration of the adults and the yellowish-green and black bands of the caterpillars serve as a warning to predators. The caterpillars are generally smooth with a pair of fleshy processes on the thorax and abdomen. The pupa or chrysalis is pale green with golden spots and hangs, suspended by the cremaster, among foliage. The monarch is a famous migrant species, travelling from Canada to California and hilly regions of Mexico where it overwinters in vast and spectacular roosts.
**Economic importance** Danaids are not pests.

WS

*Danaus plexippus*

# Blues, Coppers and Hairstreaks

**Order** Lepidoptera
**Family** Lycaenidae
**Wingspan** 15–50mm (⅝–2in)
**Distribution** Worldwide,
particularly warmer regions
**Number of species**
World–6000; NA–138; UK–18

*Lycaena phlaeas*

ws

**Identification** The species that
comprise this large family are
usually smallish butterflies. The
upper wing surfaces of males are
generally brilliantly coloured with iridescent blue, copper or
purplish scales. Some species are brownish or orange and the
females are less brilliantly coloured. The undersides of the
wings are much more dull and have small, dark-centred spots
or streaking. Many species have short curved tails on the hind
wings and all are very fragile and easily damaged. The legs are
all functional. A characteristic feature of the group is the
presence of a small notch in the margin of the eyes near the
antennae.
**Habitat** Lycaenids are widely distributed in a variety of
habitats in association with ant nests or their host plants.
**Biology** The caterpillars feed on a wide range of trees,
shrubs, herbaceous and weedy plants and nearly one third of
the known larval life histories show complex, mutualistic
associations with ant species. Some species are predacious on
aphids and coccids. The green or brown caterpillars are squat,
tapering at both ends and broad in the middle. Their legs are
concealed from view and they superficially resemble a small
slug or woodlouse. Ant-associated caterpillars secrete a special
fluid containing sugars and amino acids from abdominal
'honey glands'. The ants tolerate the caterpillars eating their
larvae or aphid herds in return for the fluid and will guard the
caterpillars ferociously. Smooth, rounded pupae can be found
on the host plant, attached by a silk belt, in debris or
underground. *Lycaena phlaeas* is the American Copper, also
known as the European Small Copper, whose caterpillars feed
on dock and sorrel plants.
**Economic importance** Predacious species are useful in
some respects. Many are very beautiful, prized by collectors
and, regrettably, close to extinction. Legislation protects many
of these butterflies around the world.

# Geometrid Moths

**Order** Lepidoptera
**Family** Geometridae
**Wingspan** 14–55mm (⅝–2in)
**Distribution** Worldwide
**Number of species** World–18,000; NA–1400; UK–270

**Identification** Species in this enormous family exhibit huge variation in form and colour. In general, the wings are rather rounded with complex patterns of fine lines and markings on a cryptic ground-colour of browns and greens. The front wing markings are carried on to the hind wings. The wings are held out horizontally or slightly swept back at rest. A few species hold their wings up in butterfly fashion. The sexes are often differently coloured and the females of some have vestigial wings. These moths have abdominal hearing organs.

**Habitat** Geometrid moths can be found everywhere.

**Biology** Adult moths are mainly nocturnal. Their elongate, slender and hairless caterpillars are cryptically coloured and recognizable by their characteristic looping motion. The caterpillars have only two pairs of abdominal prolegs, including the terminal claspers, and move by drawing their hind end up to meet the front end in a loop and then extending the head end forward. They are often called inchworms or loopers and will freeze if disturbed, assuming a twig-like appearance. Caterpillars of many species spin silk threads and descend from trees to find another host tree or to pupate in a flimsy cocoon spun between leaves or in litter. The range of plants eaten by these immature stages is immense and many species are polyphagous. *Scopula*, *Idaea*, *Eupithecia* and *Semiothisa* are a few of many widespread genera.

**Economic importance** Very many species such as the Winter Moth, *Operophtera brumata*, are serious pests of trees. Many others are agricultural and horticultural pests and can cause severe damage or defoliation.

*Biston betularia*

ws

# Lappet and Eggar Moths

**Order** Lepidoptera
**Family** Lasiocampidae
**Wingspan** Up to 100mm (4in), most under 40mm (1⅝in)
**Distribution** Worldwide except New Zealand
**Number of species** World–1500; NA–35; UK–11

**Identification** These medium to large-sized moths are very hairy and stout and the majority are yellowish-brown, brown or grey in colour with light lines across the wings and the occasional pale spot. They lack a functional proboscis and the antennae are feathery or comb-like in both sexes. Females are generally much heavier than males and have very large abdomens.
**Habitat** Lasiocampid moths are common in wooded areas, hedgerows and heathlands where their host tree species occur.
**Biology** The females are often so heavy that they cannot fly any great distance. The caterpillars, which can be quite attractively marked, are quite stout with dorsal and lateral tufts and downward-pointing hair fringes. They may live communally in silk tents or webs measuring many centimetres across, which they spin across the foliage of a wide range of coniferous and deciduous trees, grasses and low-growing herbaceous plants. The body hairs have urticating properties. When fully grown, the caterpillars pupate inside tough, papery, egg-shaped cocoons.
**Economic importance** Many lasiocampids are quite serious pests of forest and orchard trees. *Malacosoma americana*, the Eastern Tent Moth, is a pest on apple and wild cherry trees. It is very similar to the European Lackey Moth, *M. neustria*, which feeds on many tree species including hawthorn and blackthorn. The silk of lasiocampid cocoons has been used in the past but not to any great commercial extent.

*Malacosoma
neustria*

WS

# Atlas, Emperor, Moon and Royal Moths

**Order** Lepidoptera
**Family** Saturniidae
**Wingspan** 25–150mm (1–6in)
**Distribution** Worldwide, mainly tropical
**Number of species** World–1100; NA–69; UK–1

**Identification** Saturniids are very large, heavy-bodied moths with very broad, often strikingly marked wings. Many species are brightly coloured but the best examples are seen in the tropics, where wingspans may attain 200mm(8in) or more. Most species have an eyespot near the centre of each wing or transparent patches and hind wing tails. The adults have vestigial mouthparts and do not feed.

**Habitat** The adults are mainly inhabitants of wooded areas.

**Biology** The large caterpillars feed on a wide range of deciduous and coniferous trees and shrubs, the majority being host plant-specific. The surface of the caterpillars has fleshy protuberances, called scoli, which carry spines and long bristle-like hairs. The fully grown caterpillars make dense silk cocoons which can be found attached to the twigs or leaves of the host plant. The only British species is the Emperor Moth, *Saturnia pavonia*, which feeds on heather, bramble and blackthorn. Species of the genus *Attacus* can be found from South America to Mexico and from Africa to the Orient. *Samia cynthia* has been introduced from Europe to North America, where it feeds on Tree of Heaven. The green caterpillars of the spectacular green, long-tailed, Luna Moth, *Actias luna*, feed on hickory and walnut.

**Economic importance** The silk from the cocoons of many species has been used commercially.

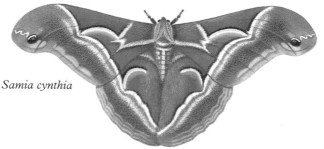

*Samia cynthia*

WS

# Hawk Moths

**Order** Lepidoptera
**Family** Sphingidae
**Wingspan** 35–150mm (1⅜–6in), most under 100mm (4in)
**Distribution** Worldwide, primarily tropical
**Number of species** World–1200; NA–124; UK–18

**Identification** Sphingids are medium to quite large, heavy-bodied moths with long, narrowish front wings. The margin of the front wings from the apex to the hind margin is very oblique or sometimes scalloped. The proboscis is very long, sometimes longer than the whole of the body, and is curled under the head when not in use. At rest, hawk moths hold their wings horizontally and raked back at a characteristic angle. Some species resemble bees and have large transparent areas of the wings devoid of scales. A few of the larger species can look like hummingbirds as they hover at flowers.
**Habitat** Hawk moths inhabit a great variety of wooded and open areas.
**Biology** The adults are fast-flying and feed on nectar which they suck from the tubes of flowers using their long probosci. Many are diurnal while others are nocturnal or fly at dusk. The herbivorous caterpillars are smooth, faintly warty and virtually all species are characterized by a terminal horn or spine-like process. Many caterpillars in this family can be very brightly coloured and patterned with short, oblique stripes, and some have anterior eyespots which have a defensive function. Most species pupate in the soil or on the ground and some have a peculiar handle which contains the proboscis.
**Economic importance** Some species are serious crop pests.

*Manduca sexta*, the Tobacco Hornworm, damages tobacco, tomato, potato and other plants in North America and other parts of the world. *Hyles lineata*, the Striped Hawkmoth, is cosmopolitan and attacks a very wide range of commercially important plants.

*Hyles lineata*

WS

# Tussock Moths

**Order** Lepidoptera
**Family** Lymantriidae
**Wingspan** 20–60mm (³⁄₄–2³⁄₈in)
**Distribution** Worldwide
**Number of species** World–2600; NA–35; UK–10

**Identification** These cryptically marked, brown, grey or whitish moths are similar to the noctuids but do not have a proboscis and do not feed. Male lymantriids tend to be a little smaller than the females and generally have different patterns on the wings. The females of some species are wingless.
**Habitat** Lymantriids can be found around hedgerows, coniferous or deciduous woods and many other habitats.
**Biology** The females are weak fliers and lay their eggs on the bark of a great variety of host trees and shrubs, often incorporating some of the hairs from the end of their abdomen. Adult and larval body hairs produce itchy rashes and serve as a protection against predators. The hairy and mostly brightly coloured caterpillars are phytophagous and are characterized by the shaving brush-like tufts or tussocks of hairs at the front, back and sometimes other regions of the body. The tufts of hair are often brightly coloured to emphasize their harmful properties. The cocoons are protected by the caterpillars weaving in their urticating hairs.
**Economic importance** The Gypsy Moth, *Lymantria dispar*, and the Brown Tail Moth, *Euproctis chrysorrhoea*, have both been introduced from Europe to North America. These two species are serious pests of all manner of tree species. Severe infestations may result in the death of the affected trees. Control attempts have included sex pheromone-baited traps and bacterial warfare against the caterpillars. Sensitive humans can develop incredible skin rashes from being in contact with lymantriids, especially the caterpillars.

*Lymantria dispar*

WS

# Tiger and Ermine Moths

**Order** Lepidoptera
**Family** Arctiidae
**Wingspan** 20–70mm (¾–2¾in), mostly 25–40mm (1–1⅝in)
**Distribution** Worldwide
**Number of species** World–2500; NA–264; UK–40

**Identification** Tiger moths are heavy-bodied, hairy and often very brightly coloured with combinations of black, red, yellow and orange. The patterning takes the form of spots, stripes or irregular patches and in some species is most pronounced on the hind wings. The colour patterns of the front wings serve to break up the outline of the body. In ermine and tiger moths (Arctiinae), the wings are held roof-like over the body at rest. Ermine moths tend to be pale or white with small black spots or patches. The family also includes the footmen moths (Lithosiinae). These moths are not heavy-bodied, are duller in colour and hold their wings flat over the body.
**Habitat** Arctiids can be found in a wide variety of habitats.
**Biology** The bright warning coloration of these mainly nocturnal moths displays their distasteful properties to predators. The adults and their hairy caterpillars are poisonous and many species feed on plants like potato, ragwort and laburnum which contain toxic substances. The caterpillars are often as brightly coloured as the adults. Many species are polyphagous and normally feed on a wide range of low-growing herbaceous plants. Footmen moth caterpillars, which are not very hairy, eat lichens on bark and rocks. The genus *Arctia*, widespread in the northern hemisphere, contains *Arctia caja*, the Garden or Great Tiger Moth.
**Economic importance** Some arctiid species can be pests of trees. The Cinnabar Moth, *Tyria jacobaea*, whose black and yellow caterpillars eat ragworts, has been introduced from Europe to North America to control Klamathweed.

*Arctia caja*

ws

# Noctuid Moths

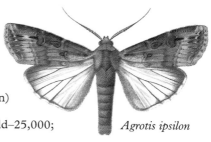

**Order** Lepidoptera
**Family** Noctuidae
**Wingspan**
15–80mm (⅝–3¼in),
mostly 20–45mm (¾–1¾in)
**Distribution** Worldwide
**Number of species** World–25,000;
NA–3000; UK–350

*Agrotis ipsilon*

ws

**Identification** Members
of this enormous family of moths are medium-sized, rather
dull coloured with narrowish front wings and broader hind
wings. The underwing moths (subfamily: Catocalinae) have
brightly coloured and patterned hind wings which, at rest, are
hidden under the cryptic front wings. Adult noctuids vary a
great deal in size and colour, but in most they have cryptic and
delicate patterns of brown, green, grey, black and white. The
antennae are hair-like in females and more brush-like in males.
The proboscis is usually well developed. The colour patterns
of both sexes are similar but males often have a tuft of hairs at
the end of the abdomen. The wings may be held roof-like over
the abdomen or flat.
**Habitat** Noctuids can be found virtually everywhere.
**Biology** These moths are nocturnal and are often attracted to
lights after dark. The adults have thoracic hearing organs and
can detect and evade bats. The caterpillars, which are dull and
cryptically marked, are elongate, stout and hairless. The
immature stages of virtually all known species are plant-,
fungus- or lichen-feeders, although a few are predacious on
small, soft-bodied insects such as coccids. The herbivorous
species may be external chewers, stem-borers or occasionally
leaf-miners. The caterpillars of many species are called
cutworms for their habit of chewing through stems at ground
level. Most noctuid caterpillars walk on their abdominal
prolegs, but in some several pairs of these prolegs are lacking
and in these cases the caterpillars move in a semi-looping
manner similar to geometrid larvae. There are very many
widespread genera, including *Spodoptera*, *Agrotis*, *Orthosia*,
*Euoxa* and *Heliothis*.
**Economic importance** It is hardly surprising that in a vast
family of herbivorous moths there are very many serious pest
species. Virtually every important crop or plant is attacked by
one or other of these moth species.

# Horntails or Woodwasps

**Order** Hymenoptera
**Family** Siricidae
**Body length** 20–40mm ($\frac{3}{4}$–1$\frac{5}{8}$in)
**Distribution** Worldwide, mainly north temperate
**Number of species** World–100; NA–20; UK–11

**Identification** Member species of this sawfly family are large, stout-bodied and reddish-brown, black or metallic blue. Some species may have striking yellow bands or greenish-purple tinges. As in all sawflies, there is no constricted waist region. A distinctive feature of these sawflies, and the reason for the common name of horntail, is the presence of a terminal abdominal spine. The spine is short and triangular in males but long and spear-like in females. Female siricids have a long and very strong ovipositor which projects below the terminal spine. The antennae are usually long and thread-like although, in some species, they may appear rather short and flattened.

**Habitat** Woodwasps are commonly found in forests.

**Biology** There are two distinct groups: species of the subfamily Siricinae attack coniferous trees, particularly pines or firs, and species of the subfamily Tremicinae attack deciduous trees such as oak, maple and elm. The long ovipositor drills through the bark into the wood where a single egg is laid. The larvae tend to burrow into heartwood. The larvae pupate in their tunnels in a cocoon of silk and chewed wood pulp. Larval development time can be two years or more. *Sirex* and *Urocerus* are widespread genera.

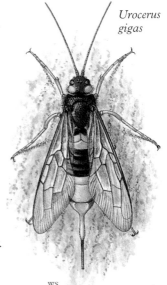

*Urocerus gigas*

**Economic importance** All species are potential pests. Woodwasps have been known to emerge from the timbers of new houses, furniture or stacked firewood. People are often alarmed by the great size and wasp-like appearance of some species but horntails do not sting.

WS

# Common Sawflies

**Order** Hymenoptera
**Family** Tenthredinidae
**Body length** 3–22mm
(⅛–¾in), most under 16mm (⅝in)
**Distribution** Worldwide, mainly
northern hemisphere
**Number of species** World–4000;
NA–735; UK–400

*Strongylogaster macula*

ws

**Identification** Common
sawflies constitute a very large
family whose species show a great diversity of structure and
habit. Species can be brown, black or green and many are
brightly patterned with yellow or red markings. Some species
may look very like wasps, but, as with all sawflies, there is no
waist. The slender antennae are variable in length and
composed of between seven and ten segments. The name
sawfly is derived from the flattened, saw-like ovipositor of the
females. In many species, the sexes have different coloration.
**Habitat** Adult sawflies can be found in nearly all terrestrial
habitats.
**Biology** The adults feed at flowers although some may be
predacious on small insects. Females use their ovipositor to
cut slits and lay eggs in the leaves, twigs and shoots of the
appropriate host plant. The larvae, which can be cryptically or
warningly coloured, are nocturnal feeders and mainly chew
foliage externally although some species are leaf-miners or gall-
makers. Most larvae look very like caterpillars but can be
distinguished by the fact that they have at least five pairs of
abdominal feet or prolegs in addition to the three pairs of
thoracic legs. The larvae feed singly or gregariously and, in
some species, can secrete a defensive fluid from special glands.
Pupation takes place in a silk cocoon or underground. There
are very many widespread genera across the northern
hemisphere including *Hoplocampa*, *Pristiphora*, *Nematus*,
*Pontania* and *Tenthredo*.
**Economic importance** Many species are pests of garden
plants, crops and trees, sometimes causing considerable
damage.

# Conifer Sawflies

**Order** Hymenoptera
**Family** Diprionidae
**Body length** 5–15mm (¼–⅝in), most under 10mm (⅜in)
**Distribution** Northern temperate regions
**Number of species** World–100; NA–41; UK–7

**Identification** These very stout-bodied sawflies are mainly dull brown or black in colour, although some may have yellowish or reddish abdominal bands and thoracic markings. The antennae of males are very broad, feathery or comb-like, whereas those of females are narrow and toothed. The abdomen is very broad across the middle and can appear slightly flattened.

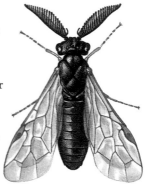

*Neodiprion sertifer*
ws

**Habitat** Conifer sawflies are confined to coniferous woods and plantations.

**Biology** The adults look rather clumsy and are slow-flying. The females of a number of species are known to produce a sexual pheromone to attract males. The feathery antennae of the males have specialized receptor cells that respond to low concentrations of the sexual scent. The majority of species attack pine trees, but a few are restricted to hemlock, firs and spruce. The larvae feed externally on the needles and can be cryptically coloured and solitary or warningly coloured and gregarious. In some species, the gregarious and conspicuously spotted larvae will jerk their bodies *en masse* if disturbed or threatened. Pupation takes place inside a tough brownish cocoon in the soil or glued to a twig or bark crevice. The two most widespread and common genera are *Diprion* and *Neodiprion*.

**Economic importance** Many species cause serious damage to their coniferous host trees, weakening or even killing them through defoliation and making them liable to viral infections. *Neodiprion sertifer* was introduced to North America from Europe.

# Stem Sawflies

**Order** Hymenoptera
**Family** Cephidae
**Body length** 4–18mm (¼–¾in), mostly 9–14mm (⅜–⅝in)
**Distribution** Mainly northern hemisphere
**Number of species** World–100; NA–12; UK–12

**Identification** Cephids are slender, cylindrical sawflies which mainly have a dull or shiny black or very dark coloration. Many species have yellow thoracic markings and abdominal bands. The antennae are quite long and thread-like and may be slightly clubbed at their ends. The prothorax is large and the abdomen is slightly flattened.

**Habitat** The slow-flying adults of this family can be found around yellow flowers in meadows and grasslands and in cereal crops.

**Biology** The larvae of all cephid species have vestigial legs and are all stem-borers in grasses, cereals, willows, raspberries and similar plants. The Wheat Stem Sawfly, *Cephus pygmaeus*, is typical. Eggs are laid in the stem and the larvae burrow up towards the ear, eating the vascular and other tissues as they go. Species of the genus *Hartigia* attack woody Rosaceae. *Cephus* and *Trachelus* species attack cereal crops.

**Economic importance** Several species are pests of wheat, barley, rye and oats. *Cephus pygmaeus* was introduced to North America from Europe in the late 1800s and has become quite a serious pest.

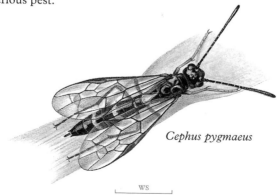

*Cephus pygmaeus*

WS

# Ichneumon Wasps

**Order** Hymenoptera
**Family** Ichneumonidae
**Body length**
3–42mm (⅛–1⅝in)
**Distribution** Worldwide
**Number of species** World–20,000;
NA–3350; UK–2000

*Rhyssa persuasoria*

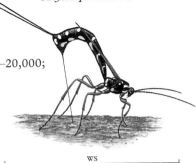

ws

**Identification** The
species in this, the largest,
hymenopteran family are
generally slender-bodied
wasps with antennae over
half as long as the body
and composed of at least 16 segments. In some species, the
middle antennal segments may be white or yellow.
Ichneumons vary enormously in size and colour. Many are
pale yellowish-brown to black, while others may be brightly
patterned with brown and black or yellow and black. The
abdomen is long and slender. The ovipositor is visible and may
be very long. Ichneumonids look similar to braconids but are
generally bigger and have different wing venation.
**Habitat** Adult ichneumon wasps are solitary, very common
and can be found almost everywhere. They are especially
attracted to umbelliferous flowers and lights.
**Biology** Adult females locate insect and spider hosts with
their antennae and use their long ovipositors to lay eggs on or
inside the body. In general, the larvae of endopterygote insects
such as butterflies, moths, beetles and flies are the main hosts
but members of other orders are also parasitized. Some species
may be host-specific, others attacking a range of insect larvae
in one type of microhabitat. Ichneumon larvae are parasitoids
and emerge from the host, usually after it has pupated. Some
species are hyperparasitoids, that is, they parasitize parasitoids.
Species of the remarkable genus *Rhyssa* parasitize the larvae of
woodwasps and beetles in timber. The ovipositor is very long
and is pushed along the host's tunnels or drilled directly
through the wood. The species of many genera such as *Pimpla*,
*Phygadeuon*, *Ophion*, *Lissonota* and *Ichneumon* are common and
widespread across the northern hemisphere. The world fauna,
if ever fully described, may exceed 50,000 species.
**Economic importance** Very many ichneumon species are of
incalculable benefit in controlling pest populations.

# Braconid Wasps

**Order** Hymenoptera
**Family** Braconidae
**Body length** 2–15mm (⅛–⅝in), most under 7mm (¼in)
**Distribution** Worldwide
**Number of species** World–15,000; NA–2000; UK–1050

**Identification** The majority of braconids are brownish, reddish-brown or black. Nearly all are small and inconspicuous and very similar in basic design to the ichneumonids. The abdomen is never particularly long, slender or laterally compressed. The identification of these and other related families of wasps is very difficult.

**Habitat** Like ichneumons, braconids can be found virtually everywhere there are insect hosts for them to parasitize.

**Biology** The vast majority of braconids are parasitoids of other insects. Very few are hyperparasitoids. The caterpillars of Lepidoptera are commonly attacked but many other orders of insects are parasitized by these wasps. Large groups of closely related braconid species tend to favour a particular type of host, some attacking aphids, others fly larvae and so on. All host stages can be attacked and the braconid females lay their eggs on or inside the body of the host. In the case of large caterpillars, many hundreds of small braconids may develop inside and spin silken cocoons on the outside of the body when they are fully grown. 'Mummified' aphids stuck to foliage are a common sight and the result of braconid attack. The mature larva emerges beneath the aphid and spins a silk cocoon which sticks the empty body of the host to the leaf. The emerging adult cuts a neat circular hole in the dried aphid corpse and flies off. Species of the genera *Bracon*, *Opius*, *Apanteles*, *Meteorus*, *Praon* and many others are widespread across the northern hemisphere. If ever fully described, this family may total some 40,000 world species.

**Economic importance** As with the ichneumons, the parasitic nature of these wasps makes them of immense value in killing pests insects. Many species are used as biological control agents against such pests as the Codling Moth, the Cabbage White Butterfly, woodworm and bark beetles.

*Apanteles glomeratus*

ws

# Platygastrid Wasps

**Order** Hymenoptera
**Family** Platygastridae
**Body length** 0.5–4mm (⅛in)
**Distribution** Worldwide
**Number of species** World–950; NA–200; UK–150

**Identification** These parasitic wasps are very small, shiny black insects with virtually no wing venation. The antennae, which have less than 11 segments, are distinctly bent or elbowed in the middle and arise close to each other and low down on the head. The ovipositor is concealed within the body when not in use and, in species of the genus *Inostemma*, the long ovipositor is contained in a bizarre forward-pointing abdominal extension.

**Habitat** Platygastrids can be found in all terrestrial habitats.

**Biology** Although the life histories of many species are unknown, nearly all of the known ones are endoparasitoids of the eggs and larvae of gall midges, mealybugs or whiteflies. Some odd examples of these wasps developing in beetle eggs and cynipid galls have been recorded. The eggs are laid in the eggs or very young larvae of the host species. Like many parasitoids, platygastrid larvae avoid eating vital organs and do not kill their hosts immediately. The host continues to grow and develop until the parasitoid pupates and emerges as an adult. Nearly half the species of this family in North America and in Britain belong to the widespread genus *Platygaster*.

**Economic importance** All species are beneficial as their hosts are almost universally pest species. Several *Platygaster* species are important control agents of the Hessian Fly (Cecidomyiidae, p.120).

*Inostemma* sp.

# Scelionid Wasps

**Order** Hymenoptera
**Family** Scelionidae
**Body length** 1–14mm (⅛–½in), most under 4mm (¼in)
**Distribution** Worldwide
**Number of species** World–1250; NA–280; UK–102

**Identification** These very small, black or rarely brownish
wasps are similar to the platygastrids but have slightly more
venation evident in the front wings. The body shape varies
from quite slender to stout. The antennae normally have 11 or
12 segments and females may have a distinct terminal club.
The antennae are bent or elbowed and arise from low on the
head. The abdomen is flattened and has sharp lateral margins.
When not in use, the ovipositor is concealed within the body
of the female.

**Habitat** Scelionids can be found in a wide variety of habitats
in association with their hosts.

**Biology** These wasps constitute a fairly large and widely
distributed group of egg parasitoids. Most adults are solitary
and lay their eggs in the eggs of Lepidoptera, Hemiptera,
Coleoptera and Orthoptera. Female scelionids avoid laying
their eggs in already parasitized host eggs by marking them
physically or with chemical odours. The scelionid larva
develops and pupates inside the host egg. Many species
require very fresh host eggs and have evolved the habit of
clinging to the adult host insect until she lays her eggs,
whereupon the scelionid female immediately inserts her own
eggs into the host egg or egg mass. Some even lose their wings
once they have located and boarded a suitable host insect.
Species of the genus *Trimorus* specialize
on beetle eggs and *Telenomus* species
parasitize moth eggs.

**Economic importance** Many species
are important in controlling natural
pest insect populations and several have
been used in biological control
programmes.

*Telenomus dalmanni*

# Gall Wasps

*Diplolepis rosae*

**Order** Hymenoptera
**Family** Cynipidae
**Body length** 1–9mm (⅛–⅜in)
**Distribution** Worldwide
**Number of species**
World–1250; NA–636;
UK–95

**Identification** Gall wasps are
shiny black or blackish-brown,
are normally fully winged, but
may be short-winged or
wingless. The female abdomen
is oval and compressed from
side to side and the thorax has a
characteristic humped
appearance. Males are usually smaller than females.
**Habitat** Gall wasps are mostly associated with oaks, with a
few species on members of the Rosaceae and Compositae.
**Biology** The vast majority of cynipid larvae are plant-feeding
gall-formers although some are non-gall-forming, sharing galls
of other species and sometimes killing the true occupant. A
few species are parasitic on the larvae or pupae of parasitic
wasps developing inside aphids. The galls of gall-forming
species are a common sight and are easier to identify than the
gall wasp that induced their growth. Adult female gall wasps
lay their eggs inside plant tissues and, by processes as yet little
understood, induce the host plant to grow a gall which
protects and nourishes the developing larvae. Galls themselves
vary enormously in size, colour, texture and location but are
always species-specific. The life-cycles can be complex, often
involving sexual and parthenogenetic generations, occurring
on different parts at different times of the year, or even, on two
different host plants. Gall wasps and their galls support diverse
communities of which parasitic wasps such as ichneumonids,
pteromalids and torymids are a large part. There are many
genera common across the northern hemisphere of which
*Diplolepis*, *Neuroterus*, *Andricus* and *Callirhytis* are notable.
*Diplolepis rosae* induces the familiar Mossy Rose or Robin's
Pincushion gall on wild roses.
**Economic importance** Galls have been used in tanning and
dyeing processes and others for medicinal purposes. Some
species can be pests, while a few have been used in the
biological control of weeds.

# Trichogrammatid Wasps

**Order** Hymenoptera
**Family** Trichogrammatidae
**Body length** 0.3–1.2mm (under ⅛in)
**Distribution** Worldwide
**Number of species** World–532; NA–43; UK–29

**Identification** There are probably many more species of these minute yellow, orange or dark brown wasps undescribed than described. Although small, many are stout-bodied. The wings are normally fully developed and have characteristic lines of small hairs in radiating patterns. The front wings are broadish and appear to have a single vein. Hind wings are smaller, narrower with a marginal fringe of hairs. Unlike other hymenopteran families, the tarsi have only three segments.

**Habitat** Trichogrammatids are present in a variety of terrestrial and aquatic habitats in association with their hosts.

**Biology** All species in this family are parasitoids of the eggs of other insects. The adult females lay their eggs inside the exposed eggs of a wide range of insect hosts. Some species cling to the body of host females to ensure their success in ovipositing on fresh eggs. Among the insect orders, the butterflies and moths, beetles, bugs, thrips, flies and other wasps are commonly parasitized. The females of some species swim under water to parasitize the eggs of aquatic insects such as water beetles and dragonflies. Larval development and pupation all takes place within the host egg and, in a few species, may be as short as three days. The adults cut their way out of the empty eggshell. To see these tiny wasps, collect insect eggs and wait to see what emerges.

**Economic importance** Many species such as *Trichogramma minutum* are used extensively as biological control agents against lepidopteran pests. However, these wasps can be pests in butterfly farms.

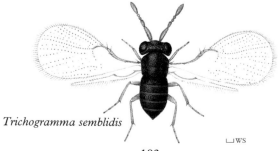

*Trichogramma semblidis*

⌐⌐WS

# Eulophid Wasps

**Order** Hymenoptera
**Family** Eulophidae
**Body length** 0.5–5mm (up to ¼in), mostly 1–3mm (⅛in)
**Distribution** Worldwide
**Number of species** World–3100; NA–510; UK–391

**Identification** The member species of this large family of small wasps are variable in shape, ranging from elongate to stout and from rounded to slightly flattened. They may be yellowish to brownish or black and may be partially or entirely metallic. The front wings are not particularly broad and they do not have hairs arranged in rows. The tarsi have more than three segments.

**Habitat** Eulophids are widely distributed in a variety of habitats dictated by the presence of their hosts.

**Biology** These wasps parasitize various species in just about all the insect orders. The range of life styles and strategies exhibited by the species in this family is very large. Most eulophids are parasitoids of hidden larvae, including the larvae of leaf-miners and gall-formers. Some species are egg parasitoids, others attack the larval or pupal stages of moths, beetles, flies, aphids, scale insects and whiteflies. A few are hyperparasitoids and parasitize the larvae of braconid or ichneumonid parasitoids inside their caterpillar hosts. Among the very many widespread genera, *Pnigalio*, *Eulophus*, *Tetrastichus* and *Pediobius* are noteworthy.

**Economic importance** The majority of species are of value in the control of natural populations of insect pests and many are used in biological control programmes. *Chrysocharis* species are used to control lepidopteran pests of larch trees and species of *Dahlbominus* have been used effectively against diprionid sawfly pests of pines. *Baryscapus bruchophagi* attacks seed chalcids in clover and alfalfa seeds.

*Baryscapus bruchophagi*

# Fairyflies

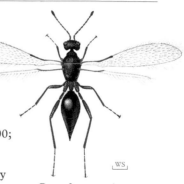

**Order** Hymenoptera
**Family** Mymaridae
**Body length**
0.2–2mm (⅛in),
mostly 0.3–1mm (under ⅛in)
**Distribution** Worldwide
**Number of species** World–1300;
NA–120; UK–87

*Caraphractus cinctus*

**Identification** Fairyflies are very small or minute wasps with yellow, dark brown or black coloration broken with pale or dark markings. No species have metallic colouring. This family contains the smallest insects on earth and some single-celled aquatic organisms are bigger than some of these wasps. The front wings, which have no obvious venation, are narrow and fringed with fine hairs. The hind wings, which are very narrow or strap-like, arise from stalks and are fringed with long hairs. The hair fringes in most species are very much longer than the width of the wing itself. The ovipositor may be concealed, visible or very long.
**Habitat** Mymarids are found in association with their hosts in terrestrial and aquatic habitats.
**Biology** These tiny wasps are all egg parasitoids of other insects. The hosts of these parasitoids occur in many orders, including the Odonata, Orthoptera, Psocoptera, Thysanoptera, Lepidoptera, Coleoptera and Diptera, but nearly half the known life histories show that planthopper eggs and the eggs of related homopteran bug familes are the main targets. The females insert their eggs into fresh host eggs and the further development of the host is arrested. The females of *Caraphractus cinctus* swim, using their wings as paddles, to reach the eggs of giant water beetles and can remain submerged for days at a time. Species of *Anagrus*, *Ooctonus*, *Gonatocerus* and *Polynema* occur across the northern hemisphere.
**Economic importance** Several species have been used successfully as biological control agents of insect pests.

# Torymid Wasps

**Order** Hymenoptera
**Family** Torymidae
**Body length** 1–10mm (⅛–⅜in),
most under 5mm (¼in)
**Distribution** Worldwide
**Number of species** World–1500;
NA–175; UK–75

*Torymus
varians*

WS

**Identification** The body of these wasps is
elongate and usually highly metallic blue or
green in colour. The thorax is weakly
sculptured with small dimples and the
abdomen is normally smooth. The jaws are
very strong and toothed. The antennae are
elbowed and have 13 segments. The venation of the wings is
very reduced. The coxa of the hind legs is many times larger
than the coxa of the front legs. The femur of the hind legs may
have one or more tooth-like projections. The ovipositor is
always visible and can be as long as the rest of the body or
even longer.
**Habitat** The species that constitute this family can be found
in all manner of habitats, in association with their hosts.
**Biology** Torymids vary as much in biology as they do in
appearance and they may be predacious or herbivorous as
larvae. A large number of species are parasitoids of gall-
forming Diptera and Hymenoptera although some may simply
consume the gall tissue without damaging the occupant. The
females use their long ovipositors to drill through the woody or
spongy tissue of the gall to reach the host larvae developing
inside. Other torymid species attack caterpillars, the eggs of
mantids and the larvae of some solitary bees and wasps. The
herbivorous torymids are all confined to the rich nutrient
resources provided by the seeds of a wide range of plants. In
these species the female lays her eggs directly into the seeds of
coniferous, hawthorn, apple, pear and related tree species. The
larvae generally eat the entire contents of the seed. Species of
the large and widespread genus *Torymus* are typically parasitic
whereas species of *Megastigmus* feed in the seeds of conifers
and members of the Rosaceae. The rearing of galls in small
containers will almost always provide some torymids for
examination.
**Economic importance** Insect-eating species can be
beneficial but seed-feeding species can be pests.

# Pteromalid Wasps

**Order** Hymenoptera
**Family** Pteromalidae
**Body length** 1–8mm (⅛–⅜in), most under 5mm (¼in)
**Distribution** Worldwide
**Number of species** World–3100; NA–400; UK–532

**Identification** Although there are many undescribed species, all known pteromalids are black or very metallic blue or green. These wasps are very variable in appearance and the body shape varies from elongate and slender to moderately robust. The antennae have between 8 and 13 segments. The thorax is usually large and covered with small dimples and the abdomen is smooth. The hind coxae are not enlarged and the hind femora do not have teeth. The vast majority are fully winged and have reduced venation.

**Habitat** Pteromalids are found everywhere in association with their insect hosts.

**Biology** The majority of species are parasitoids or hyperparasitoids, a few are gall-formers, herbivores or are directly predacious on small insects such as gall midge larvae or the eggs of other insect species. The life-histories of pteromalids are very varied indeed and the larvae or pupae of a large range of host insects including flies, beetles, wasps, butterflies, moths and fleas are attacked. Female pteromalids may lay their eggs on or in their hosts and drill through plant tissue to reach gall-forming, leaf-mining or stem-boring hosts. Some species lay one egg, while others may lay hundreds of eggs in a suitably sized host. Many genera are widespread and common across the northern hemisphere. *Pteromalus*, *Habrocytus*, *Mesopolobus* and *Trichomalus* are typical.

**Economic importance**
Beneficial as natural predators of pest species. Some are cosmopolitan such as the useful *Choetospila elegans* whose larvae are parasitoids of bruchid, drugstore and grain beetles. Another worldwide species is *Nasonia vitripennis* whose larvae destroy house flies and related species. Some species are used as biological control agents of crop pests.

*Pteromalus dolichurus*

WS

# Encyrtid Wasps

**Order** Hymenoptera
**Family** Encyrtidae
**Body length**
0.5–4.5mm (up to ¼in),
mostly 1–2mm (⅛in)
**Distribution** Worldwide
**Number of species**
World–3000; NA–500; UK–201

*Habroletis
dalmani*

**Identification** These wasps are
small, yellowish-orange, red,
brown or a variety of metallic shades. Most species are stout
although some can be quite slender or flattened. The antennae
have up to 15 segments in females but only up to 10 segments
in males. The thorax is convex and the front and middle legs
have a tibial spur. The middle legs are used for jumping and
the spur on these legs is large. Most species are fully winged
with reduced venation but short-winged and wingless species
occur. The ovipositor may be concealed or visible.

**Habitat** Encyrtids can be found everywhere in association
with their hosts.

**Biology** Although the majority of these wasps are parasitoids
of the immature stages and adults of scale insects, mealybugs,
aphids and whiteflies, they have been recorded attacking
species in just about every insect order. Some species are
parasitoids of caterpillars and the larvae of weevils, and other
species are hyperparasitoids of the larvae of pteromalids,
braconids and even other encyrtids. Polyembryony is an
interesting feature of some of these wasps. The eggs laid by the
females divide repeatedly at an early stage of their
development to produce anything from ten to a couple of
thousand larvae from a single egg. *Encyrtus*, *Blastothrix* and
*Copidosoma* are just a few of the genera common to both sides
of the Atlantic.

**Economic importance** Species in this family are among the
most important biological control agents and many have been
used successfully against serious pests. *Habrolepis dalmani* has
been used to control a very serious oak-feeding scale insect
and several other encyrtids have been of great value in
controlling citrus pests.

# Ruby-tailed, Cuckoo or Jewel Wasps

**Order** Hymenoptera
**Family** Chrysididae
**Body length** 3–18mm (⅛–¾in), mostly under 12mm (½in)
**Distribution** Worldwide
**Number of species** World–3000; NA–230; UK–33

**Identification** Chrysidids are incredibly beautiful and very metallic coloured insects. The body can be bright blue, green, red or combinations of these colours. The body surface is extremely hard to protect them from bee and wasp stings, and is strongly sculptured with coarse pits and dimples. A good recognition feature is that the underside of the abdomen is nearly always concave, enabling them to curl up into a ball if attacked. Only three or four abdominal segments are visible from above, the rest being telescoped. The females have an ovipositor which can be retracted and a secondary structure or sting which is, in most cases, not functional and venomless.

**Habitat** Adult chrysidids feed at flowers and can be seen, especially on hot days, investigating the nests and holes of solitary bees and wasps.

**Biology** The name cuckoo wasp refers to the habit of many of these insects whose larvae are parasitic or eat the nest provisions left by the host bees or wasps. Some species are parasitic on sawfly larvae or pupae and a few eat the eggs of mantids. In the general case, the female chrysidid lays her eggs in the ground, wood cavity or mud cell nests of solitary bee or wasp species. The hatched chrysidid larva may eat the host larva but always consumes its paralyzed insect food supply. *Chrysis fuscipennis* parasitizes potter wasps of the genus *Eumenes* and digger wasps of the genus *Sceliphron*. *Chrysis* is the largest genus across the northern hemisphere.

*Chrysis
fuscipennis*

**Economic importance** A few may be beneficial in destroying sawflies but the majority might be considered a nuisance as they kill useful bees and wasps.

WS

# Spider-hunting Wasps

**Order** Hymenoptera
**Family** Pompilidae
**Body length** 5–55mm (¼–2¼in), mostly 15–25mm (⅝–1in)
**Distribution** Worldwide
**Number of species** World–4000; NA–290; UK–41

**Identification** Pompilids can be smallish to quite large and are all dark-coloured, blue or black usually with dark yellowish, bluish or black wings. A few species may have yellowish or orange markings. The body is slender and the legs, especially the hind legs, are long and spiny. The wings are not folded back over the body at rest. Males are smaller and more slender than the females. The antennae are quite long and, in females, often curl after death. The best recognition feature is the way they run over the ground in an agitated manner, continuously flicking and jerking their wings.
**Habitat** Adults are quite common and can be found at flowers or on the ground in open, dry, sandy areas.
**Biology** Pompilids are active hunters, rarely flying, but running rapidly over the ground in search of spiders to paralyze and use as food provision for their larvae. The venom of these fierce wasps is strong enough to overcome even the largest of spiders. The females make mud nests in crevices, dig burrows underground or simply use the host spider's own burrow. Once the spider is paralysed, the female lays an egg on it and inters it. Some prepare their nests before catching spiders, others afterwards and some cheat by laying their eggs on the paralysed spider of another wasp before it is sealed in. When the larva has eaten all the food, it pupates in the nest and the emerging adult uses its strong jaws to escape.
**Economic importance** The venom of these wasps can be very strong and stings are often extremely painful.

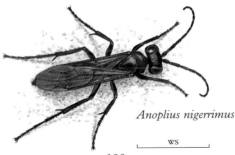

*Anoplius nigerrimus*

WS

# Velvet Ants

**Order** Hymenoptera
**Family** Mutillidae
**Body length** 3–25mm (⅛–1in)
**Distribution** Worldwide
**Number of species** World–5000; NA–480; UK–3

**Identification** Although these wasps are certainly velvety and some are very ant-like, they are not ants. Mutillids are black or reddish-brown in colour with spots or bands of red, yellow or silver short hairs. The body surface has a sculpturing of coarse dimples. The sexes of a given species are often very differently marked. The males are fully winged but the wingless females, who are strongly built, have a modified, non-segmented, box-like thorax.

**Habitat** The males of some species are found at flowers, the females are most commonly seen running over the ground in dry, shady or open locations. Some species are nocturnal.

**Biology** These interesting insects are parasitic on the larvae and pupae of various wasps and bees which develop in soil, wood or paper nests. Species of the genus *Mutilla* specialize on bumble bees of the genus *Bombus* while others attack a wider range of hosts, including halictid bees and pompilid and sphecid wasps. In the typical case, female mutillids locate and bite open a host cell and investigate the contents. If the larva inside is too young, the cell is resealed; however, if the occupant is a fully developed larva or prepupa, an egg will be laid on it before the cell is sealed. The mutillid larva hatches, eats the contents and pupates in a tough cocoon within the host's cell. In North America, *Dasymutilla* is a very large and widespread genus whose members are inappropriately called cow or mule killers. Some species, if disturbed, can make squeaking noises.

**Economic importance** Female mutillids have very powerful stings which can be most painful.

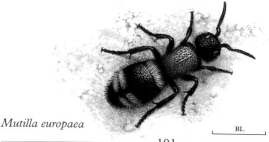

*Mutilla europaea*

BL

# Tiphiid Wasps

**Order** Hymenoptera
**Family** Tiphiidae
**Body length** 4–30mm (¼–1¼in)
**Distribution** Worldwide
**Number of species** World–1500; NA–225; UK–3

**Identification** Tiphiids are quite slender, shiny, yellowish-brown and black, or black wasps. The body is slightly hairy and the legs are short, spiny and red, yellow or black coloured. The males of all species are fully winged and usually have a short upturned spine at the end of the abdomen. Females can be fully winged or wingless. The underneath of the middle thoracic segment has two lobes which may cover the coxae of the middle legs. The waist may be very strongly constricted.
**Habitat** Adults can be found feeding on nectar at flowers or on honeydew. The females can be seen running over the ground. Some species are nocturnal.
**Biology** All known tiphiids are parasitic on the larvae of beetles, bees and wasps. Males of some species are rare, the females reproducing by parthenogenesis. Females of the genus *Tiphia* dig in soil to locate the larvae of scarab beetles. When hosts are located, the female wasp will break open the cell, sting the beetle grub and may chew it with her mandibles before laying her egg. The wasp leaves, sealing the cell behind her. Females of the genus *Methocha* are very ant-like and specialize in parasitizing tiger beetle larvae within their burrows. *Tiphia intermedia*, an American species, attacks scarab beetles of the genus *Phyllophaga*. In Europe, *T. femorata* parasitizes the larvae of dung beetles and cockchafers.
**Economic importance** Some species have been investigated as potential biological control agents.

*Tiphia intermedia*

ws

192

# Ants

**Order** Hymenoptera
**Family** Formicidae
**Body length**
1–20mm (⅛–¾in)
**Distribution** Worldwide
**Number of species** World–8800;
NA–600; UK–42

*Lasius niger*

⌊BL⌋

**Identification** These insects are familar and ubiquitous. Ants may be pale yellow, reddish through all shades of brown to black. Individuals commonly seen are wingless workers. The second or second and third abdominal segments are constricted to form the petiole or waist. The head is modified according to caste and species and may be very large with massive or specialized jaws. The antennae are elbowed immediately after the long first segment. Some ants have stings while others are modified to spray formic acid or other repellant substances.

**Habitat** Ants can be found in every type of terrestrial habitat.

**Biology** Ants are highly social insects with separate castes for different jobs within their colonies. Unlike wasps and bees, there are no solitary species. Worker ants are wingless, sterile females while the queens and males, who form mating swarms at certain times of the year, are winged. After mating, males die and females lose their wings. Colonies, which may have one or more egg-laying queens, vary greatly in size and architecture. Nests may be above or underground, they may be anything from great mounds of coniferous needles and gigantic subterranean chambers to small nests in natural cavities. Ants can be herbivorous, carnivorous or omnivorous and many are 'addicted' to the honeydew produced by aphids and the special sweet substances produced by many species of insect and plant with whom they have evolved symbiotic relationships. The common names for various groups, such as leaf-cutting, weaver, fungus-growing harvester, bulldog, army and slave-making ants, reflect the diverse biology of these fascinating insects. Ants produce a number of species-specific chemical secretions for colony regulation, trail-making, alarm-raising, defence and attack. The genera *Formica*, *Lasius* and *Myrmica* are widespread and common in the northern hemisphere. There may be twice as many or more world species than already described.

**Economic importance** Although many species are pests, ants are a vital component of every terrestrial ecosystem.

# Common, Paper and Potter Wasps

**Order** Hymenoptera
**Family** Vespidae
**Body length** 8–25mm (³/₈–1in)
**Distribution** Worldwide
**Number of species** World–3800; NA–415; UK–30

**Identification** This large family has several distinct subfamilies: Vespinae (yellow jackets and hornets), Masarinae (masarine wasps), Eumeninae (potter wasps) and Polistinae (paper wasps). The species in this family will be recognized by everyone as 'wasps' and the majority are black with characteristic yellow or white markings. Paper wasps are usually brown with a few yellow markings. With the exception of the masarine wasps, wings are folded in longitudinal pleats and held at the sides of the abdomen.
**Habitat** Vespids can be found in virtually every kind of terrestrial habitat. Yellow jackets and paper wasps are a common sight in summer and early autumn.
**Biology** Yellow jackets, hornets and paper wasps are social insects living in colonies with a queen, males and sterile worker females. Potter wasps and masarines are not social. Yellow jackets and hornets make nests of paper from chewed wood fibres, inside which there may be thousands of workers. The colonies last one year and the larvae are reared on chewed insects. The adults feed on nectar and other sugar-rich materials. Species of the genus *Vespula* make underground nests while species of *Dolichovespula* tend to nest in bushes or trees. The potter wasps, which are sometimes considered to be a separate family, make small nests in the ground or in stems or vase-shaped nests of mud or clay. The nests are stocked with paralyzed caterpillars and an egg is suspended from the roof before it is sealed. *Eumenes* is a typical and widespread genus.
**Economic importance** Female vespids have a powerful sting and the venom can cause intense pain. Many species are useful as predators of caterpillars.

ws

*Vespula germanica*

# Solitary Hunting, Digger and Sand Wasps

*Ectemnius cephalotes*

**Order** Hymenoptera
**Family** Sphecidae
**Body length** 2–44mm (⅛–1¾in)
**Distribution** Worldwide
**Number of species** World–8000; NA–1140; UK–115

WS

**Identification** Members of this large family exhibit a great diversity of appearance. The body varies from black with yellow or reddish markings to metallic green or blue with yellowish or reddish markings. The head is relatively broad. The antennae are 12-segmented in females and 13-segmented in males. The hairs of the body are simple and not branched or feathery as in bees. In some species the abdomen is very elongate and thread-like at the front end where it joins the thorax. Females often have a toothed, comb-like, digging structure on the front legs.

**Habitat** Adult sphecids feed at flowers and other sources of sugary liquids and many species are active in bright sunshine around sandy, open localities.

**Biology** Sphecids are solitary wasps who nest in the ground, rotten wood, hollow stems, in the burrows of other insects or construct mud cells in a variety of situations. The common names for various subgroups such as digger wasps, sand-loving wasps, organ-pipe wasps and mud-dauber wasps, reflect their different habits. The larvae are carnivorous on insects or spiders paralyzed or killed and sealed in the nest by the females. Insect prey of many orders is used, but normally each sphecid species restricts itself to a single type of prey item. Species of *Ammophila* and *Crossocerus* catch caterpillars, *Trypoxylon* and *Sceliphron* species catch spiders, *Bembix* and *Crabro* species catch flies and so on. Some species may use one single large prey item while others may use several small ones. A few species are parasitic and lay their eggs in already provisioned nests of other sphecids. There are several genera common to both sides of the Atlantic.

**Economic importance** Many species control natural insect populations, some of which may be pest species.

# Plasterer and Yellow-faced Bees

**Order**  Hymenoptera
**Family**  Colletidae
**Body length**  3–18mm (⅛–¾in), most under 13mm (⅝in)
**Distribution**  Worldwide, mainly southern hemisphere
**Number of species**  World–3000; NA–155; UK–20

**Identification**  Colletids are generally slender to moderately robust, very dark or black bees with no distinct markings and sparse light golden or whitish body hairs. The abdominal hairs are often arranged in conspicuous bands. Some species have yellow or pale facial markings and may be relatively bare. A powerful hand lens will be needed to see the branched or feathered body hairs, which are characteristic of these and all other families of bees. The tongue is short and broad.

**Habitat**  These bees are common and can be found at flowers where they feed on pollen and nectar.

**Biology**  The species in this family are solitary, make very simple nests and are considered to be primitive. Plasterer bees make their nests in natural cavities in stones, bricks and similar places or in the ground in sandy locations. They use a special secretion from an abdominal gland to line the interior of their cells. This secretion dries to form a waterproof, cellophane-like film. Yellow-faced bees nest in the pith of plant stems or the empty burrows of wood-boring insects. Plasterer bees transport pollen on their hind legs while yellow-faced bees ingest the pollen and transport it in their crops. The larval cells are provisioned with a runny mixture of regurgitated pollen and honey. The large plasterer bee genus, *Colletes*, and the yellow-faced bee genus, *Hylaeus*, are typical of the northern hemisphere. Some authors consider this and all following bee families to be subfamilies of the Apidae.

**Economic importance**
These bees are valuable plant pollinators.

*Hylaeus bisinuatus*

WS

196

# Sweat Bees

*Halictus rubicundus*

**Order** Hymenoptera
**Family** Halictidae
**Body length** 4–15mm (¼–⅝in),
most under 10mm (⅜in)
**Distribution** Worldwide
**Number of species**
World–5000; NA–502; UK–58

ws

**Identification** Most of these
small to medium-sized bees are
brownish or black and some may
have a metallic blue or green
appearance or be entirely shiny
bluish-green. The surface of the
body is not generally very hairy
and may have sculpturing in the form of pits or dimples. Some
species can be confused with members of the Adrenidae but
the abdomen of halictids is more cylindrical. Another feature
separating the two families is that, in halictid bees, there is a
single groove under the socket of each antenna, whereas in
andrenid bees, there are two grooves. The tongue is short and
pointed.

**Habitat** Adults can be found everywhere, in flower-rich
meadows, woodland edges and around waste ground.

**Biology** The name of sweat bee is not appropriate to the
whole family as only a few species (*Lassioglossum*) are attracted
to sweat in addition to their normal diet of pollen and nectar.
They will sting if squeezed between folds of the body or
clothing but the sting is not very painful. Halictids are of
interest because, although many are solitary, other species
exhibit a range of social development. Most species make nests
in the ground or in burrows and many prefer clay-rich or
sandy locations. The nests usually take the form of a single,
nearly vertical burrow with or without lateral tunnels. Brood
cells are arranged in dense clusters on all the tunnels. The cells
are lined with the same secretions as used by colletid bees,
which serve to waterproof the interior and inhibit the growth
of fungi. The genera *Halictus*, *Lassioglossum* and *Nomia* are
typical and occur across the northern hemisphere. Species of
the genus *Sphecodes* are cuckoo bees, being parasitic in the
nests of other halictids.

**Economic importance** Many species are important plant
pollinators. *Nomia melanderi*, the Alkali Bee, is managed in
North America for alfalfa pollination.

# Mining or Andrenid Bees

**Order** Hymenoptera
**Family** Andrenidae
**Body length** 4–20mm (¼–¾in), mostly 10–15mm (⅜–⅝in)
**Distribution** Worldwide except Australia
**Number of species** World–4000; NA–1200; UK–67

**Identification** The bodies of andrenids can be reddish-brown, brown or brownish-black. Some species are yellow marked or entirely yellow and a few are white. Body hairs may be white, yellow or golden. The thorax may be densely hairy and the abdomen, which is often rather flat in appearance, may have transverse bands of hairs or be relatively bare. There are two grooves beneath each antennal socket as compared with only one groove in the halictids. The tongue is short and pointed. Many species may look superficially like honey bees.
**Habitat** Adrenids can be found in any flower-rich habitat.
**Biology** Sometimes called solitary mining bees, many species in this family are common springtime insects. The females make nests in soil burrows but often nests occur in large groups or aggregations. Pollen is collected and transported in the scopa of the hind legs which is formed by a dense fringe of branched hairs. The larval cells are provisioned with a pasty mixture of pollen and honey moulded into a pea-shaped pellet. Many species of andrenid are restricted to a few closely related species of flower. Some bees of the family Anthophoridae are parasitic in the nests of some andrenids. Andrenid bees are also common victims of Strepsiptera. Most species in this family occurring in North America, Britain and the rest of the northern hemisphere belong to the genus *Andrena*.
**Economic importance** Andrenids are major pollinators of spring flowers.

*Andrena clarkella*

ws

# Leaf-cutter and Mason Bees

**Order** Hymenoptera
**Family** Megachilidae
**Body length** 7–21mm (¼–¾in)
**Distribution** Worldwide
**Number of species** World–3000;
NA–682; UK–40

**Identification** The member species of this very large family of bees are generally stout-bodied, medium-sized and exhibit a range of body colours.

*Megachile centuncularis*
‌ws

Many species are dark brown to black and may have bright yellow or pale markings. Mason bees of the genus *Osmia* are short and broad with metallic blue or green coloration. The wings may be clear or smoky and the tongue is long and pointed. The females of pollen-collecting species do not carry their pollen loads on the hind legs but in a brush of stiff hairs on the underside of the abdomen.

**Habitat** Megachilids are common everywhere, particularly in areas where there is a supply of dead wood or pithy plant stems to provide nest sites.

**Biology** The majority of species are solitary bees, nesting in natural cavities in the ground, dead wood, hollow stems, snail shells and similar ready-made places. Unlike other solitary bees, megachilids do not line their brood cells with glandular secretions. Instead they collect materials such as mud, resin, leaf matter and animal or plant hairs. Leaf-cutter bees (*Megachile* spp.) are named for the habit of using their mandibles to cut neat circular pieces of leaves or petals to line the larval cells. The cells are arranged in rows and lines to fill the nest cavity. Other species such as those of *Anthidium* and *Callanthidium* are often called carder bees because they use their jaws to strip the hairs from woolly-leaved plants which they tease out to make cell linings. Species of *Osmia* and allied genera make mud cells under stones, in ground burrows or even inside empty plant galls. Not all megachilids make nests and provision their larvae with food supplies of pollen and honey. Species of *Stelis* and *Coelioxys* are parasitic in the nests of megachilid and some other bees.

**Economic importance** Like all bees, megachilids are important plant pollinators. The Alfalfa Leaf-cutter Bee, *Megachile rotundata*, was accidentally introduced from Eastern Europe to North America where it is now managed commercially for alfalfa pollination.

# Digger, Cuckoo and Carpenter Bees

**Order** Hymenoptera
**Family** Anthophoridae
**Body length** 3–28mm (⅛–1¼in)
**Distribution** Worldwide
**Number of species** World–4200; NA–920; UK–43

**Indentification** The family is a large one and contains many
bee species of diverse appearance. The cuckoo bees
(subfamily: Nomadinae) are black and yellow or brown and
white. Cuckoo bees do not have pollen baskets, are relatively
hairless and often wasp-like. Digger bees (subfamily:
Anthophorinae) may be stout and hairy or bare. The body
colour in this group varies from pale brown, yellowish and red
to black and the various species show a variety of markings or
abdominal banding. The carpenter bees (subfamily:
Xylocopinae) may be very large, hairy, blackish or bluish
species or small, relatively bare, dark bluish-green species.
Female digger and carpenter bees have densely hairy pollen
scopae on their hind legs.
**Habitat** These bees are found virtually everywhere in flower-
rich localities.
**Biology** Anthophorids are mainly fast-flying, solitary bees
although a few species show a small degree of social behaviour.
Species of *Nomada* and related cuckoo bees are parasitic in the
nests of bees of all other families except the Megachilidae and
Apidae. Digger bee species such as those in the genus
*Anthophora* dig burrows in the ground and provision their
larval cells with a mixture of pollen and honey. Carpenter bees
of the genus *Xylocopa* make nests by excavating solid wood
(often in structural timbers) whereas species of the genus
*Ceratina* excavate the pith of plant stems to make nests.
**Economic importance** Anthophorids are valuable
pollinators.

*Anthophora furcata*

ws

# Bumble and Honey Bees

**Order** Hymenoptera
**Family** Apidae
**Body length** 3–27mm (⅛–1¼in)
**Distribution** Worldwide
**Number of species** World–1000;
NA–57; UK–27

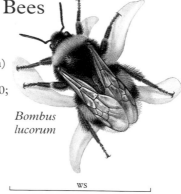

*Bombus lucorum*

ws

**Identification** Bumble bees
are very hairy, stout-bodied,
brownish-orange to black with
yellow markings. Body hairs can
be a variety of colours but
yellow, orange or yellow and
black are typical. Honey bees are smaller, more slender and
golden brown with pale hairs. The females of most species
have a specialized pollen basket, the corbiculum, on the outer
surface of each of the hind tibiae.

**Habitat** These bees can be seen everywhere visiting flowers of
all kinds. Bumble bees are particularly common at higher
latitudes and in mountainous regions.

**Biology** Apids are highly social insects who live in complex
and often very large colonies with a queen, males and sterile
worker females. Bumble bees (*Bombus* spp.) form annual
colonies with only mated queens surviving the winter months.
The nests may be under or on the ground and are made of
grass with internal, wax-constructed brood cells. The larvae
are fed on pollen and honey. Workers are reared first to build
up the colony, males appearing later in the summer. Species of
the genus *Psithyrus* are parasites, laying eggs in nests of other
bumble bees, whose workers then rear the 'cuckoos'. Honey
bees belong to the genus *Apis* and the best known of the seven
species is the Western Honey Bee, *A. mellifera*, which has been
spread by commerce throughout the world. Honey bees are
the most highly evolved of all social insects. Each colony
comprises a single egg-laying queen, many tens of thousands
of workers and up to 2,000 males or drones. The nest is a
vertical array of double-sided wax combs divided into
thousands of hexagonal cells. Cells are used for rearing young
and as pollen and honey stores. Workers use a special dance
language to communicate the distance, quality and direction of
food sources. Colony defence is co-ordinate by pheromones.

**Economic importance** Apids are major crop pollinators.
The value of crops pollinated by honey bees alone far exceeds
the value of the honey, wax and products they provide.

# Glossary

Many unfamiliar words used in entomology may be found in dictionaries, but for convenience the most common terms are listed here. Those words *italicized* are also defined.

**Apodous** Without legs.
**Aposematic** Having bright coloration to serve as a warning to *predators*. Usually red, yellow and black.
**Apterous** Lacking wings.
**Biological control** The use of natural predators, parasites or disease-producing organisms to effect a reduction in the populations of pest species.
**Caste** Any group of individuals in a colony of social insects that are structurally or behaviourally different from individuals in other groups, i.e. soldiers, workers, reproductives as seen in termites, bees and ants.
**Chrysalis** The alternative name for a lepidopteran pupa.
**Class** A taxonomic subgroup, above Order, below Phylum.
**Cocoon** A silk case made by the fully-grown larvae of many insects just before pupation.
**Corbiculum** The pollen basket of honey bees, being a concave, shiny area on the hind tibiae, fringed with stiff hairs, and capable of carrying large pollen loads.
**Cosmopolitan** Occurring throughout most of the world.
**Cryptic** Of coloration, designed to blend with background.
**Cuckoo** A term used for an insect who uses food stored by another to rear her own young.
**Dimorphic** Occurring in two distinct forms. The sexes of some insects are differently coloured or shaped.
**Dorsal** The upper or back surface of a structure or animal.
**Elytra** (*sing.* **elytron***)* The rigid front wings of beetles, modified as covers for the hind wings and not used in flight.
**Endopterygota** (*adj.* endopterygote) Insects with wings that develop internally. Metamorphosis is complete and there is a pupal stage (*holometabous*).
**Exopterygota** (*adj.* exopterygote) Insects with wings that develop outside the body. Metamorphosis is incomplete and there is no pupal stage (*hemimetabolous*).
**Family** A taxonomic group below that of Order and composed of subfamilies, genera and species.
**Gall** An abnormal plant growth caused by a virus, bacterium, fungus, mite or insect.
**Genitalia** The hard parts of insects' reproductive systems that engage between males and females during mating.

**Hemimetabolous** Developing by incomplete or gradual metamorphosis such as in the Orthoptera and Hemiptera. Immature stages are called nymphs (see *exopterygota*).

**Holometabolous** Developing by complete metamorphosis such as in the Diptera and Lepidoptera. Immature stages are called larvae (see *endopterygota*).

**Hyperparasitoid** A *parasitoid* of another parasitoid.

**Inquiline** A species that lives in the nest, gall or home of another.

**Monophagous** Restricted to eating a single species plant or type of foodstuff.

**Oligophagous** Restricted to eating a small range of related plants or foodstuffs (see *polyphagous, monophagous*).

**Omnivorous** Having variable eating preferences.

**Parasite** (*adj.* parasitic) A species living off the body or tissues of another but not causing the death of the host.

**Parasitoid** A species living off the body or tissues of another and causing the death of the host species.

**Parthenogenesis** (*adj.* parthenogenetic). Reproduction without the need for fertilization by males.

**Pheromone** A volatile substance produced by insects to communicate with others for the purposes of reproduction, aggregation, defence.

**Phloem** The main transport vessels of plants taking nutrients from the leaves to other parts.

**Phytophagous** Eating plants (also, herbivorous).

**Polymorphic** Having more than two forms.

**Polyphagous** Eating a wide range of plants or foodstuffs.

**Predacious** (*n.* predator) Eating other animals.

**Pronotum** The dorsal cover of the first segment of the thorax.

**Saprophagous** Eating decayed organic material.

**Spiracle** The breathing holes of insects leading to the tracheae occurring at the sides of the abdomen and thorax.

**Sting** The modified ovipostor of some Hymenoptera used for injecting venom.

**Stridulation** The act of producing sound, usually by rubbing two parts of the body together.

**Subfamily** A taxonomic subdivision of *family*.

**Symbiosis** Different species living in an association which brings mutual benefit.

**Tracheae** (*sing.* trachea) The internal airways of insects.

**Vector** An intermediate host which carries a disease organism in contact with its target organism.

**Ventral** The under or lower surface of a structure or animal.

**Xylem** The vessels of a plant, carrying water from the roots to other parts.

# Bibliography

Arnett, R. H. Jr, *American Insects: A Handbook of the Insects of America North of Mexico* (Van Nostrand Reinhold, New York, 1985)

Borror, D. J. & White, R. E., *A Field Guide to the Insects of America North of Mexico* (Houghton Mifflin, Boston, 1970)

Chapman, R. F., *The Insects: Structure and Function*, 3rd edn. (English University Press, London, 1982)

Chinery, M., *Collins Guide to Insects of Britain and Western Europe* (Collins, London, 1986)

Daly, H. V., Doyen, J. T. & Ehrlich, P. R., *Introduction to Insect Biology and Diversity* (McGraw-Hill, New York, 1978)

O'Toole, C. (ed.), *The Encyclopaedia of Insects* (Allen and Unwin, London; Facts on File, New York, 1986).

Richards, O. W. & Davies, R. G., *Imm's General Textbook of Entomology*, 10th edn, 2 vols (Chapman and Hall, London, 1988)

# Acknowledgments

I thank my friends and colleagues in Oxford and at the Natural History Museum for discussion and advice. A few specimens were borrowed from other institutions and I am grateful to Dr Ian Gauld (Natural History Museum), Dr William Foster (Department of Zoology, Cambridge University), Dr John Maunder (Medical Entomology Centre, Cambridge University), John Lane (London School of Hygiene and Tropical Medicine) and Professor Michael Hassell (Imperial College, Silwood Park).

# Index